ADAMTINE

Also by Hannah Berry:

Britten and Brülightly

HANNAH BERRY

ADAMTINE

Jonathan Cape
London

Published by
Jonathan Cape 2012
2 4 6 8 10 9 7 5 3 1

First published in Great Britain in 2012 by
Jonathan Cape
Random House,
20 Vauxhall Bridge Road,
London SW1V 2SA

www.vintage-books.co.uk

 ISBN 9780224089081

 Addresses for companies within The Random House Group Limited can be found at:
www.randomhouse.co.uk/offices.htm

 The Random House Group Limited Reg. No. 954009

A CIP catalogue record for this book is available from the British Library

 Printed and bound in China by C & C Offset Printing Co., Ltd

DEDICATIONS

FOR MUM
And her own unnerving ghost stories

FOR DAD
Who unwittingly instilled the fear (it's OK, I forgive you)

FOR CHRIS
With whom I shared all the terrors of childhood

Whistleblower

Delegator

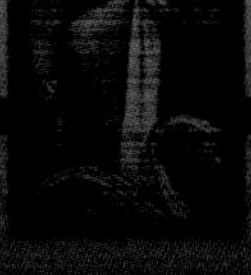

SPECIAL THANKS DUE

Nigel Baldwin ↑

Emily Gravett ↑

Dan Franklin ↗

Xavier Beyaert →

Prevaricator

Bystander

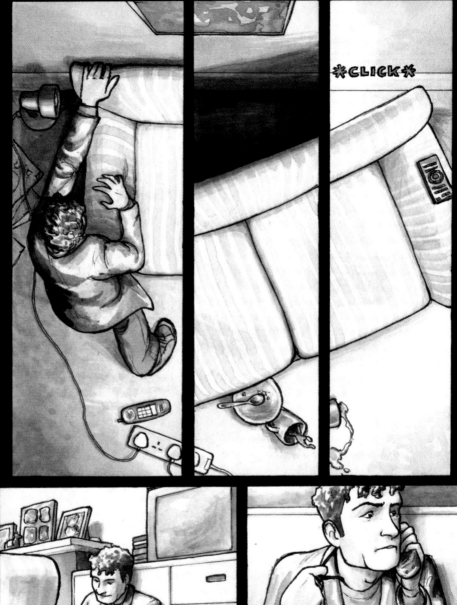

CLICK

IT'S ME.
ARE YOU
THERE
YET?

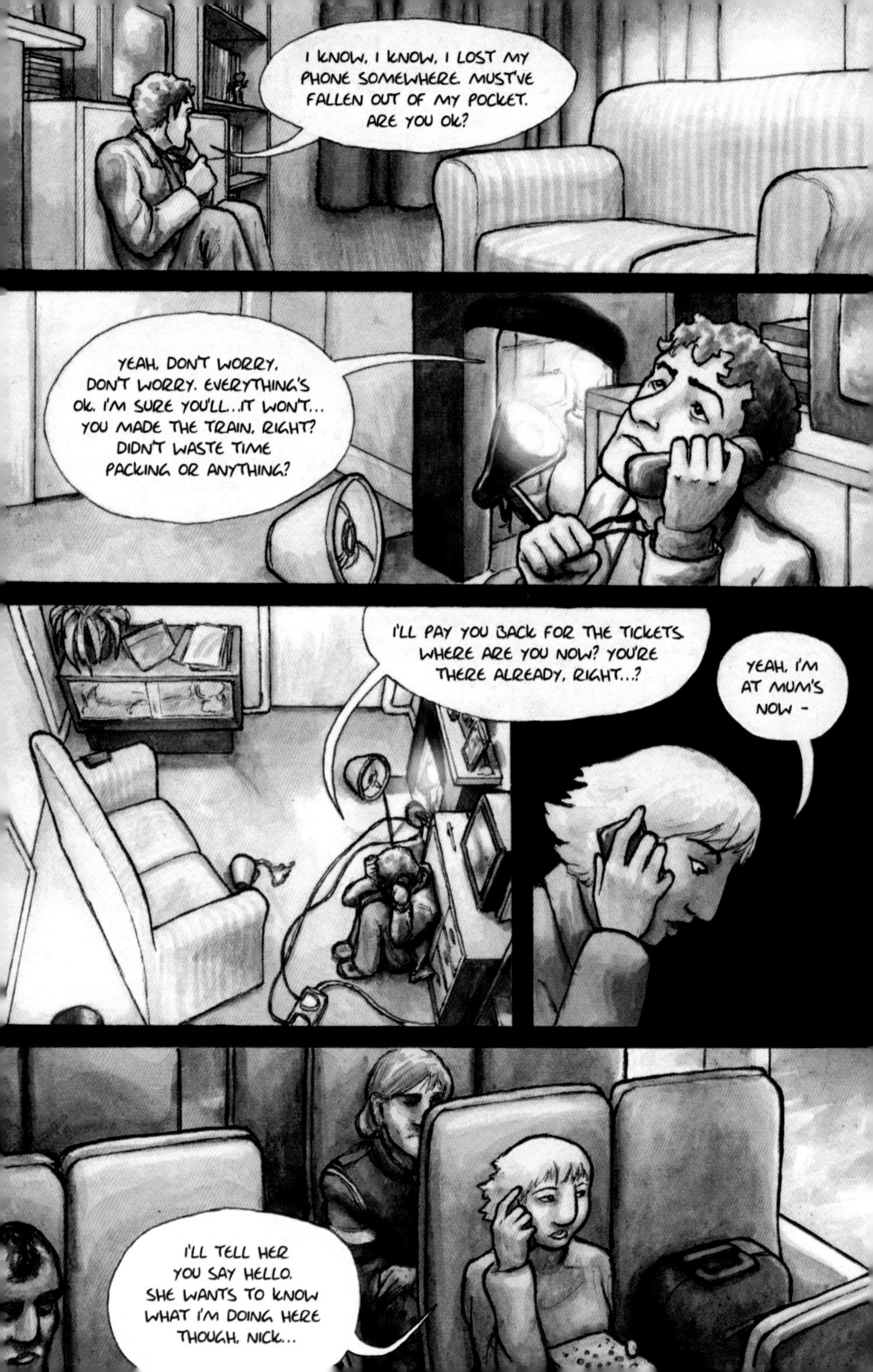
I KNOW, I KNOW, I LOST MY PHONE SOMEWHERE. MUST'VE FALLEN OUT OF MY POCKET. ARE YOU OK?
YEAH, DON'T WORRY. DON'T WORRY. EVERYTHING'S OK. I'M SURE YOU'LL...IT WON'T... YOU MADE THE TRAIN, RIGHT? DIDN'T WASTE TIME PACKING OR ANYTHING?
I'LL PAY YOU BACK FOR THE TICKETS. WHERE ARE YOU NOW? YOU'RE THERE ALREADY, RIGHT...?
YEAH, I'M AT MUM'S NOW -
I'LL TELL HER YOU SAY HELLO. SHE WANTS TO KNOW WHAT I'M DOING HERE THOUGH, NICK...

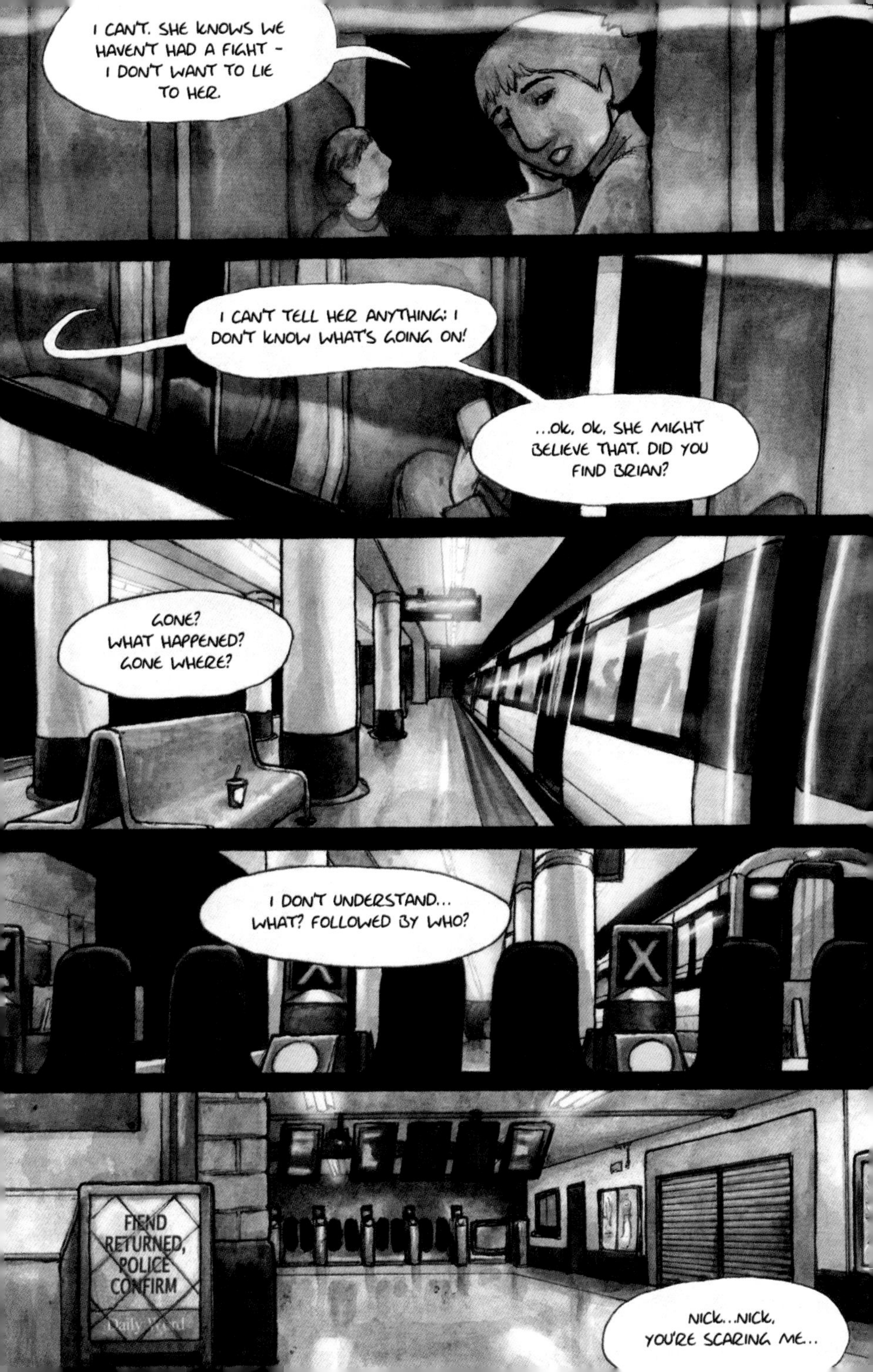
I CAN'T. SHE KNOWS WE HAVEN'T HAD A FIGHT - I DON'T WANT TO LIE TO HER.
I CAN'T TELL HER ANYTHING: I DON'T KNOW WHAT'S GOING ON!
...OK, OK, SHE MIGHT BELIEVE THAT. DID YOU FIND BRIAN?
GONE? WHAT HAPPENED? GONE WHERE?
I DON'T UNDERSTAND... WHAT? FOLLOWED BY WHO?
FIEND RETURNED, POLICE CONFIRM
Daily Word
NICK...NICK, YOU'RE SCARING ME...

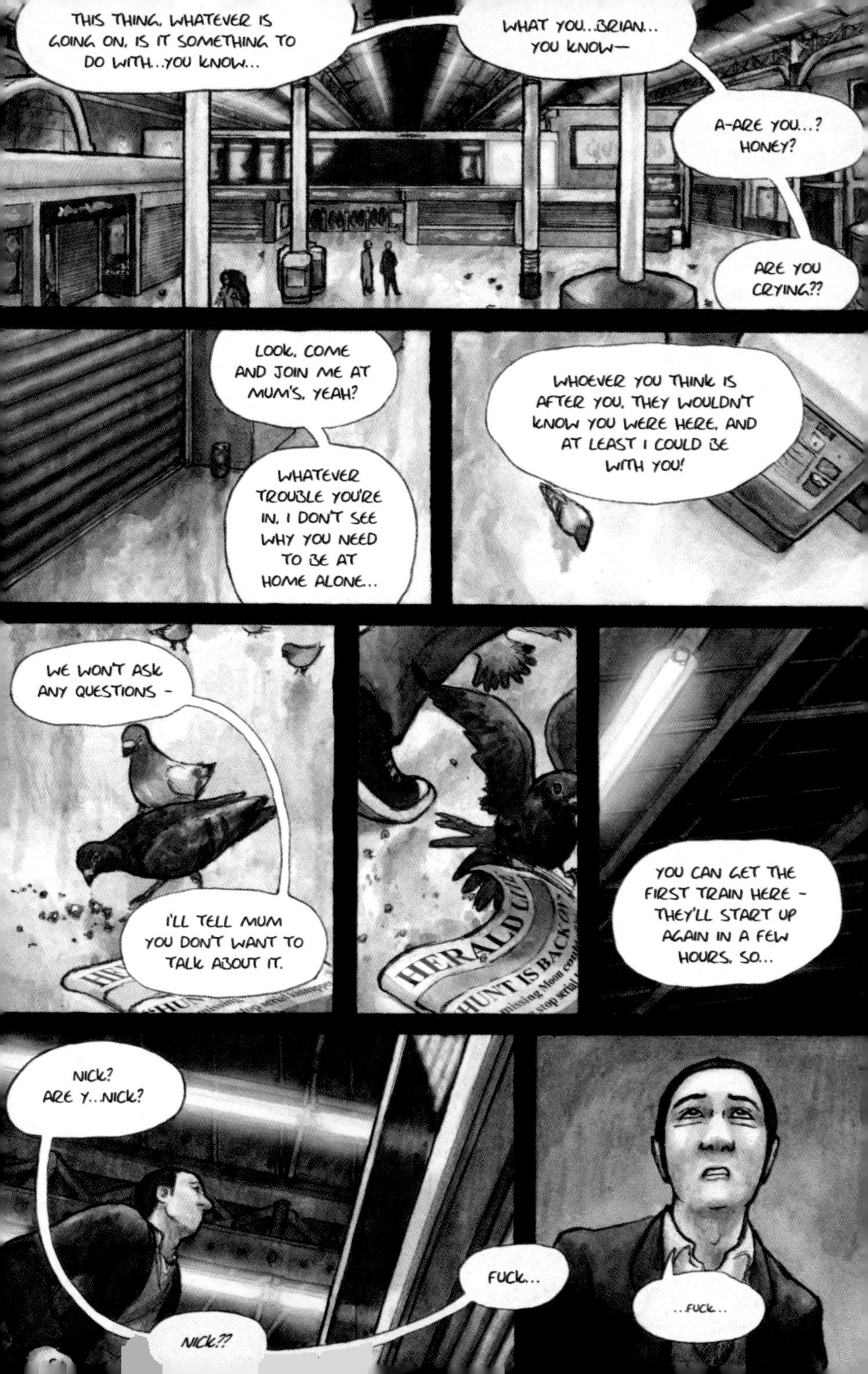
THIS THING, WHATEVER IS GOING ON, IS IT SOMETHING TO DO WITH...YOU KNOW...
WHAT YOU...BRIAN... YOU KNOW—
A-ARE YOU...? HONEY?
ARE YOU CRYING??
LOOK, COME AND JOIN ME AT MUM'S, YEAH?
WHATEVER TROUBLE YOU'RE IN, I DON'T SEE WHY YOU NEED TO BE AT HOME ALONE...
WHOEVER YOU THINK IS AFTER YOU, THEY WOULDN'T KNOW YOU WERE HERE, AND AT LEAST I COULD BE WITH YOU!
WE WON'T ASK ANY QUESTIONS -
I'LL TELL MUM YOU DON'T WANT TO TALK ABOUT IT.
HERALD
HUNT IS BACK
YOU CAN GET THE FIRST TRAIN HERE - THEY'LL START UP AGAIN IN A FEW HOURS, SO...
NICK? ARE Y...NICK?
NICK??
FUCK...
...FUCK...

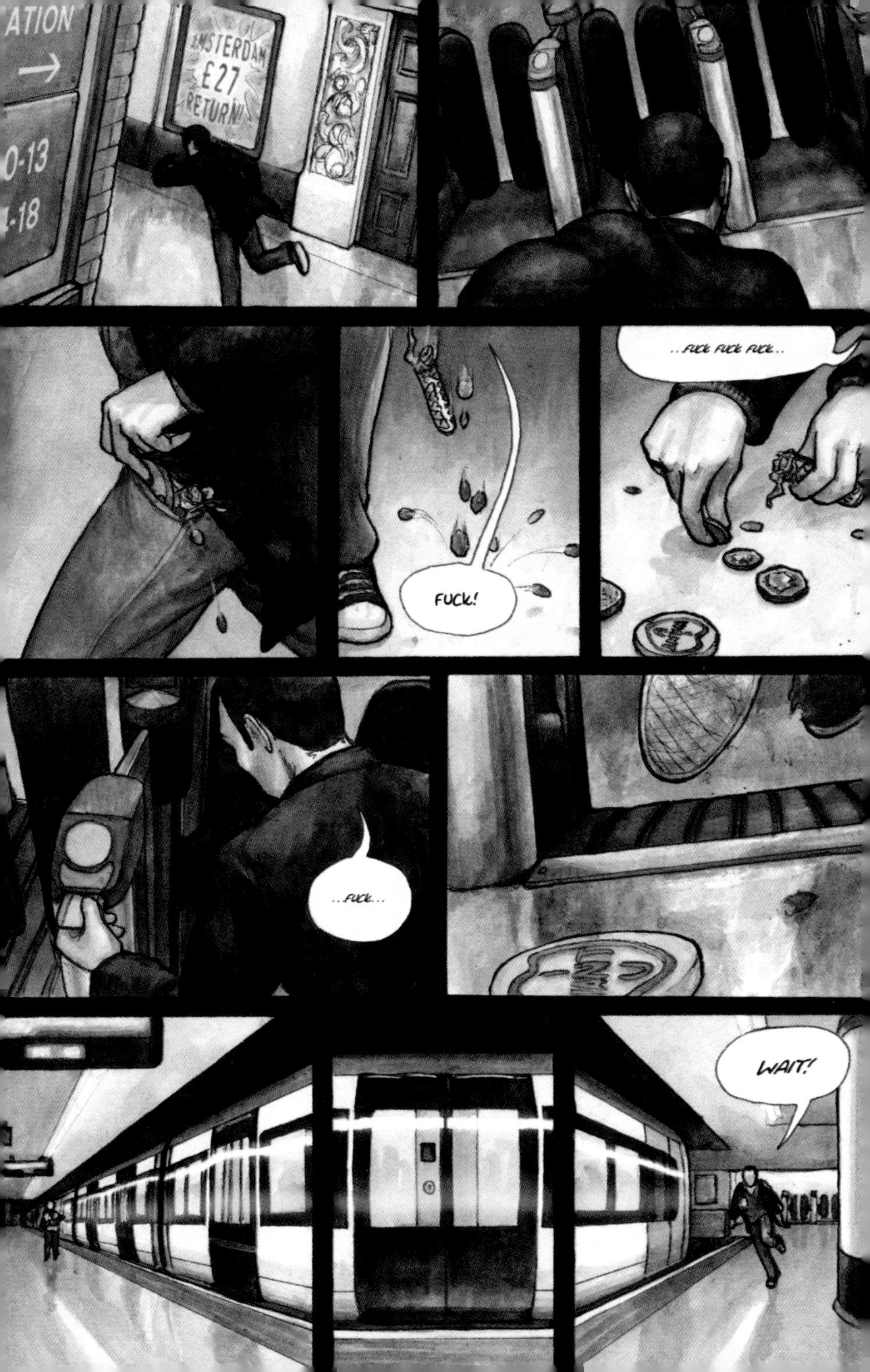
ATION
0-13
-18
AMSTERDAM £27 RETURN!
FUCK!
...FUCK FUCK FUCK...
...FUCK...
WAIT!

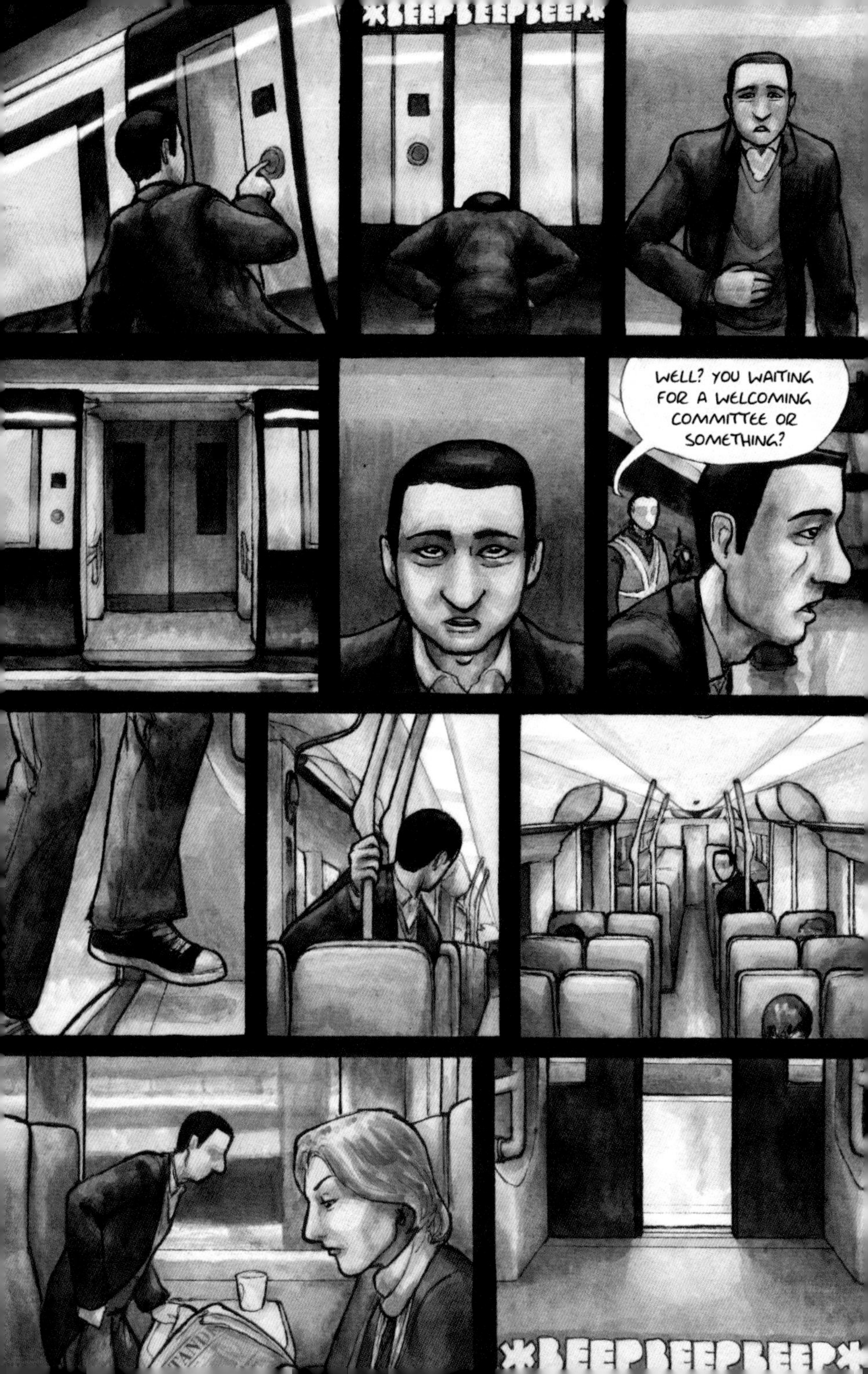
BEEPBEEPBEEP
WELL? YOU WAITING FOR A WELCOMING COMMITTEE OR SOMETHING?
BEEPBEEPBEEP

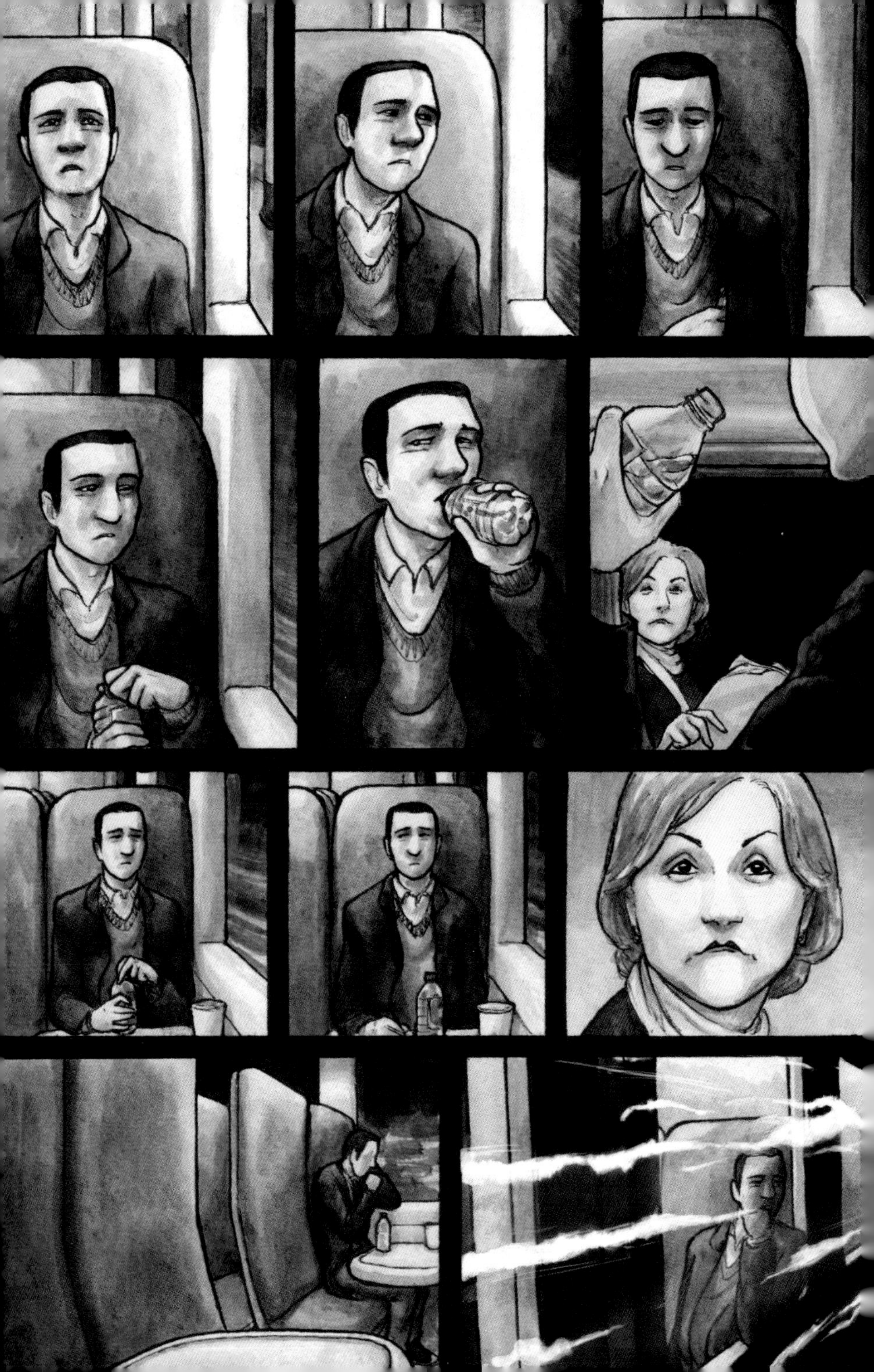

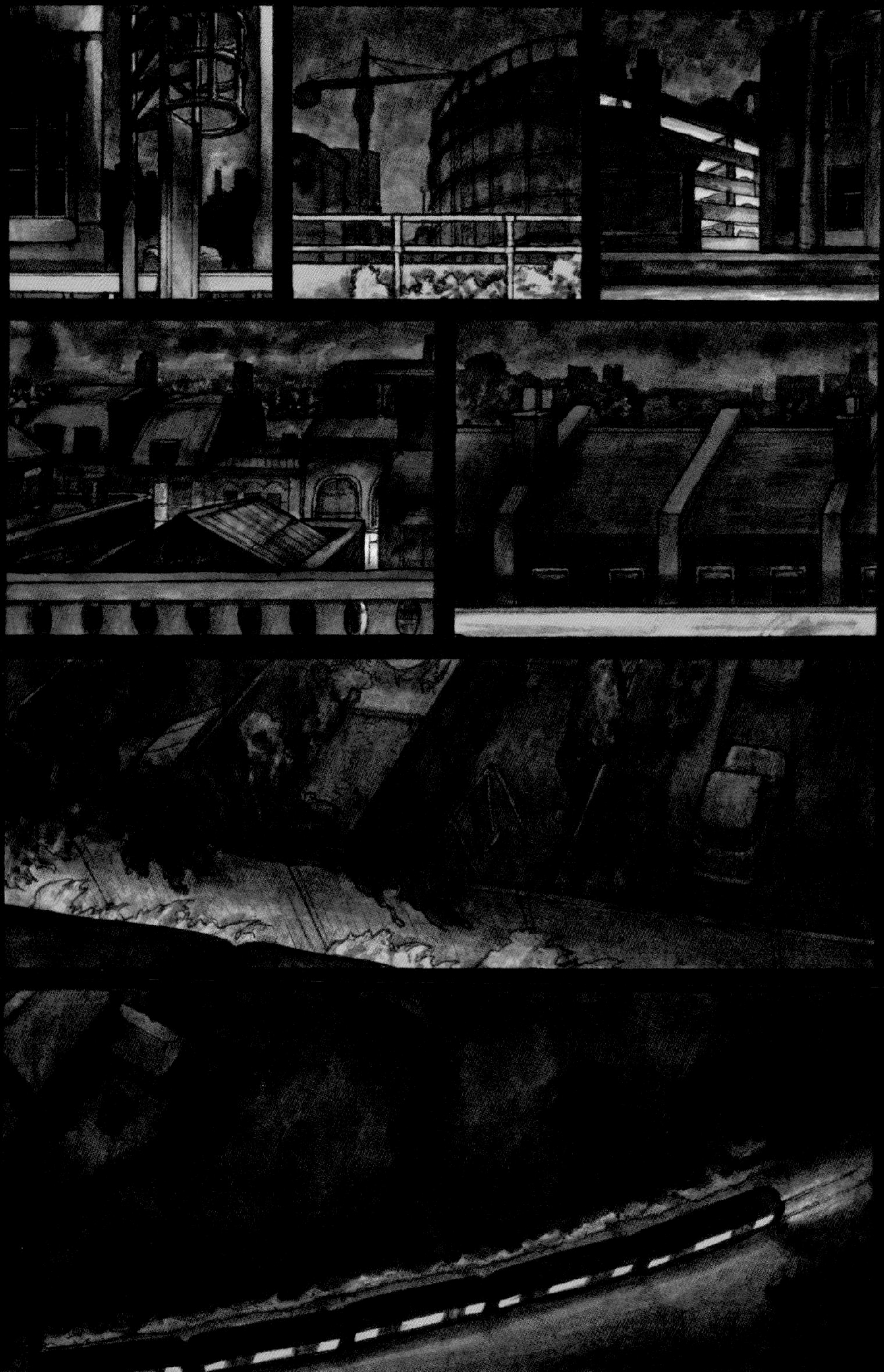

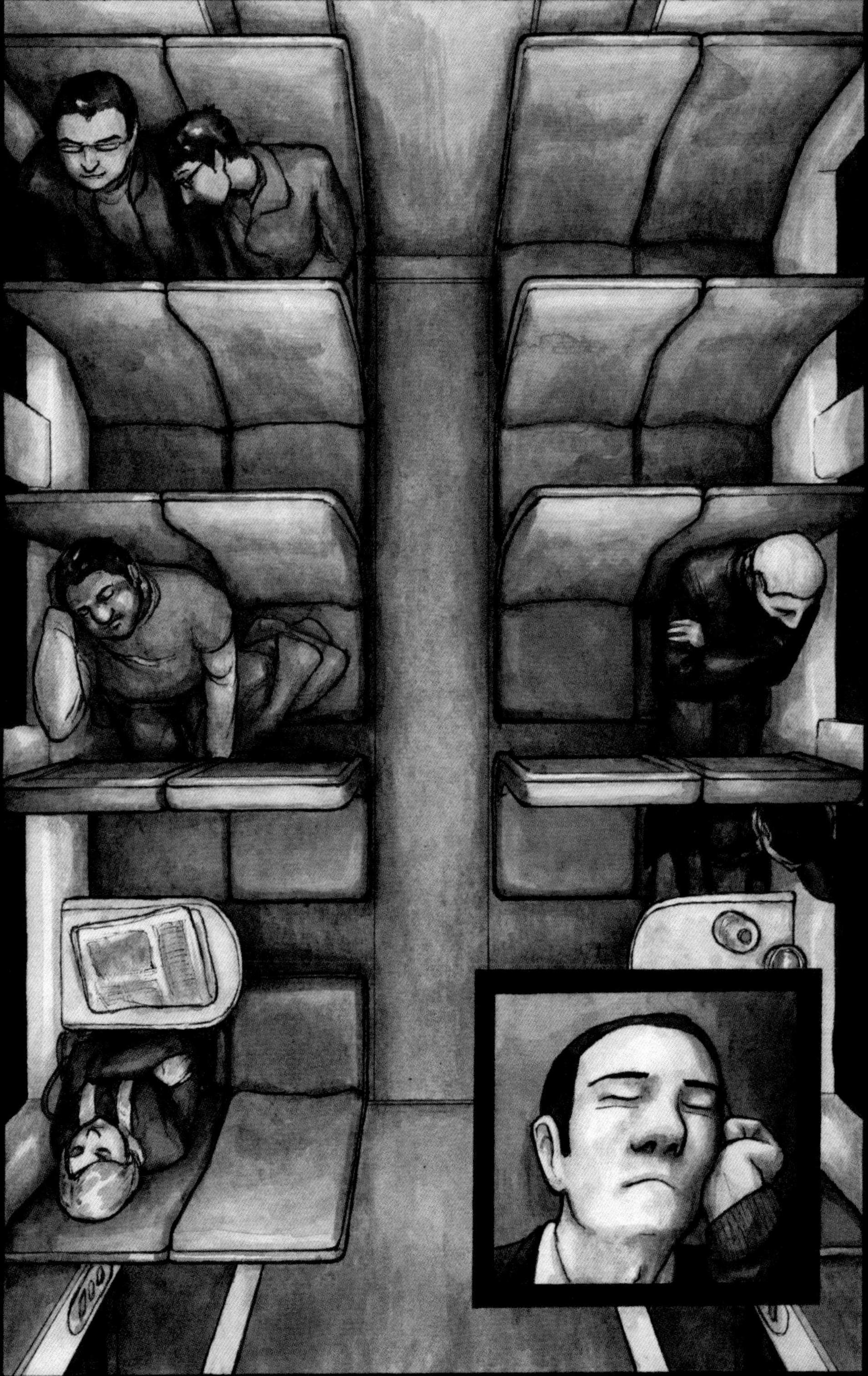

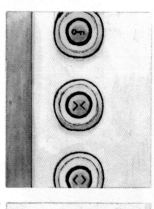

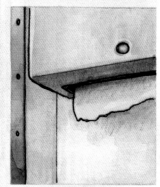
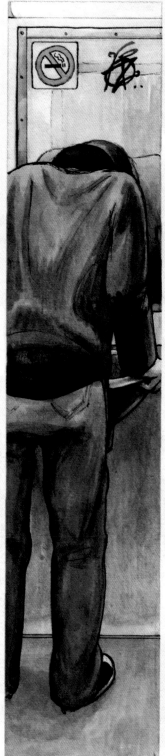

Now wash
your hands

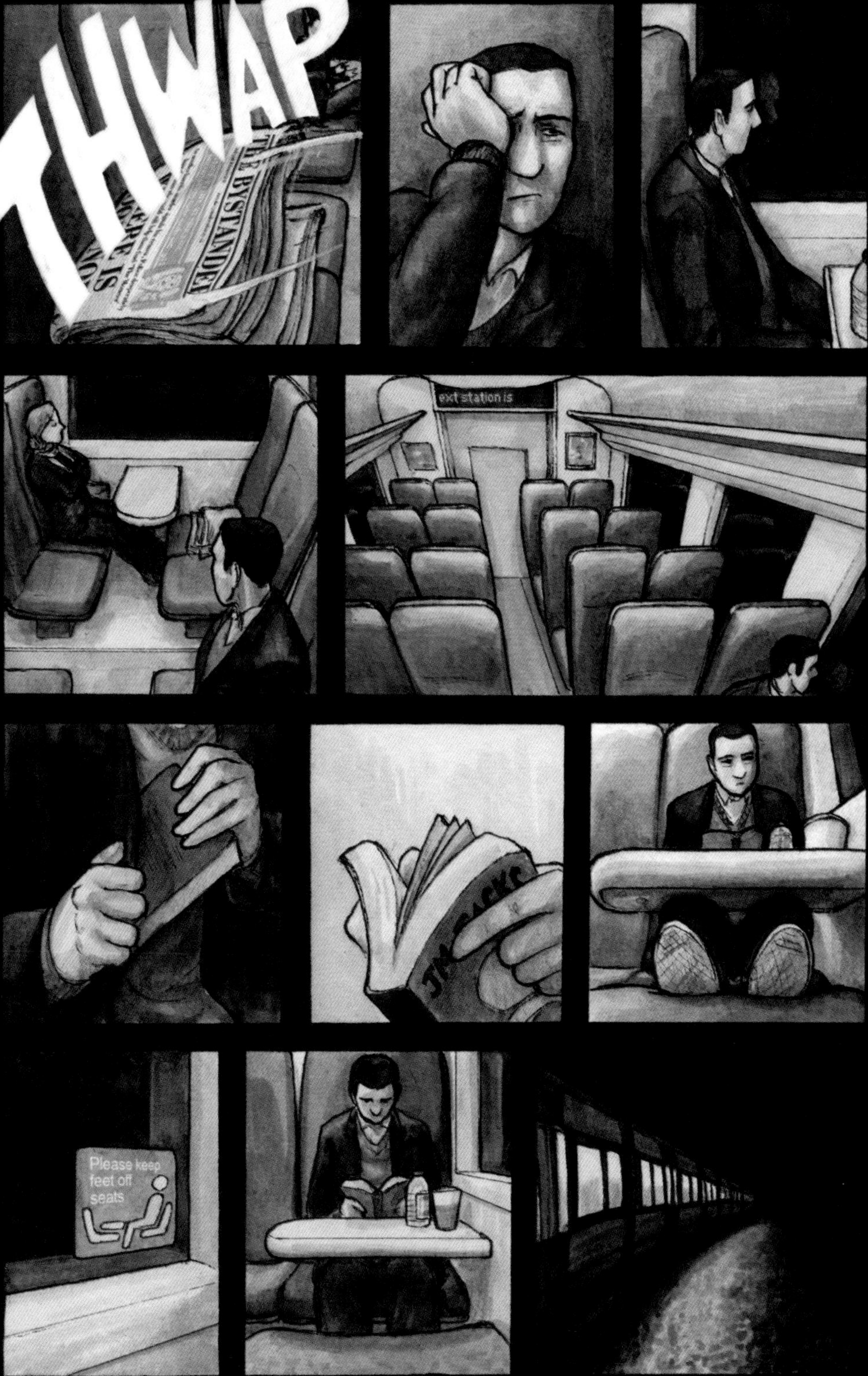
THWAP
ext station is
Please keep feet off seats

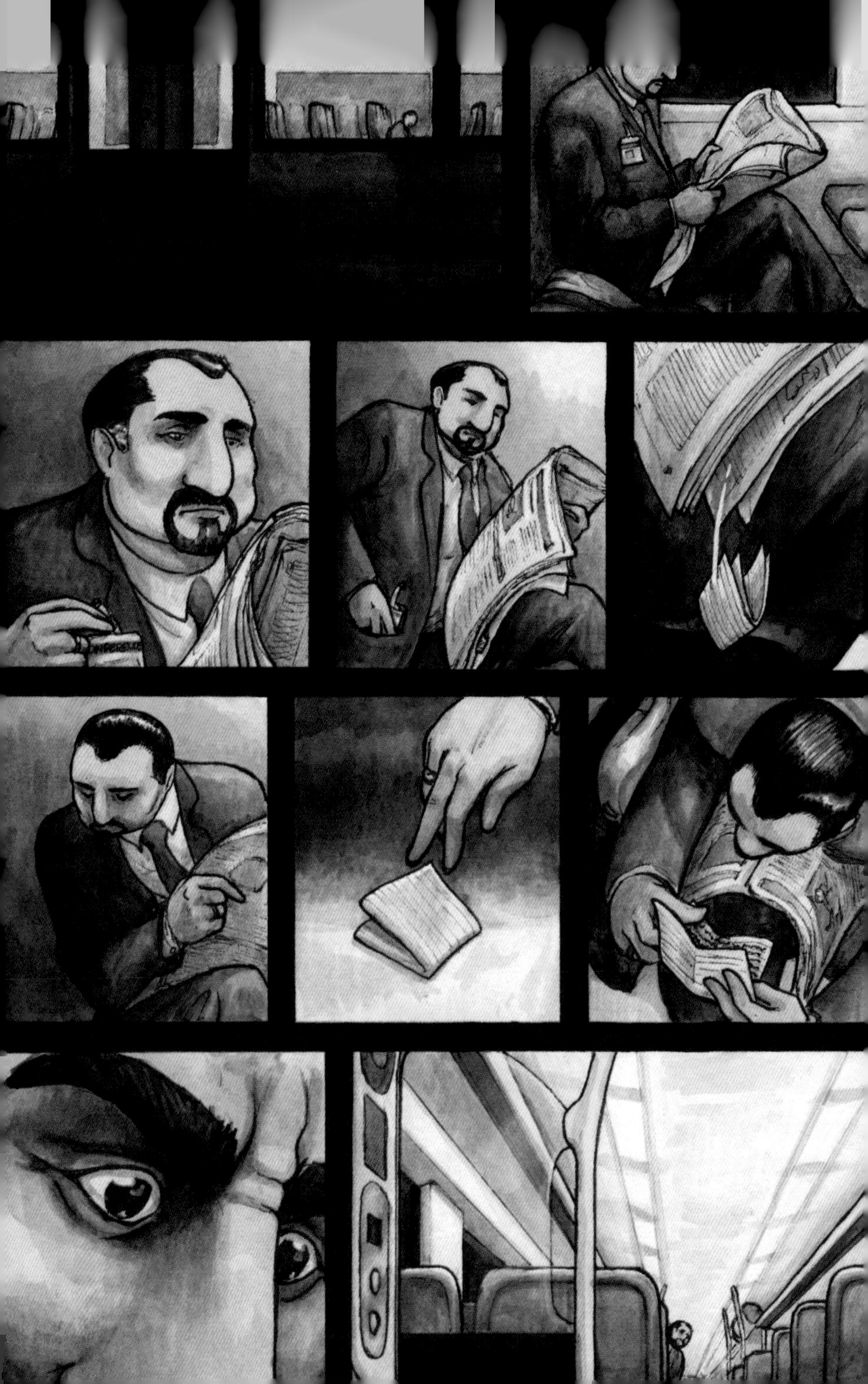

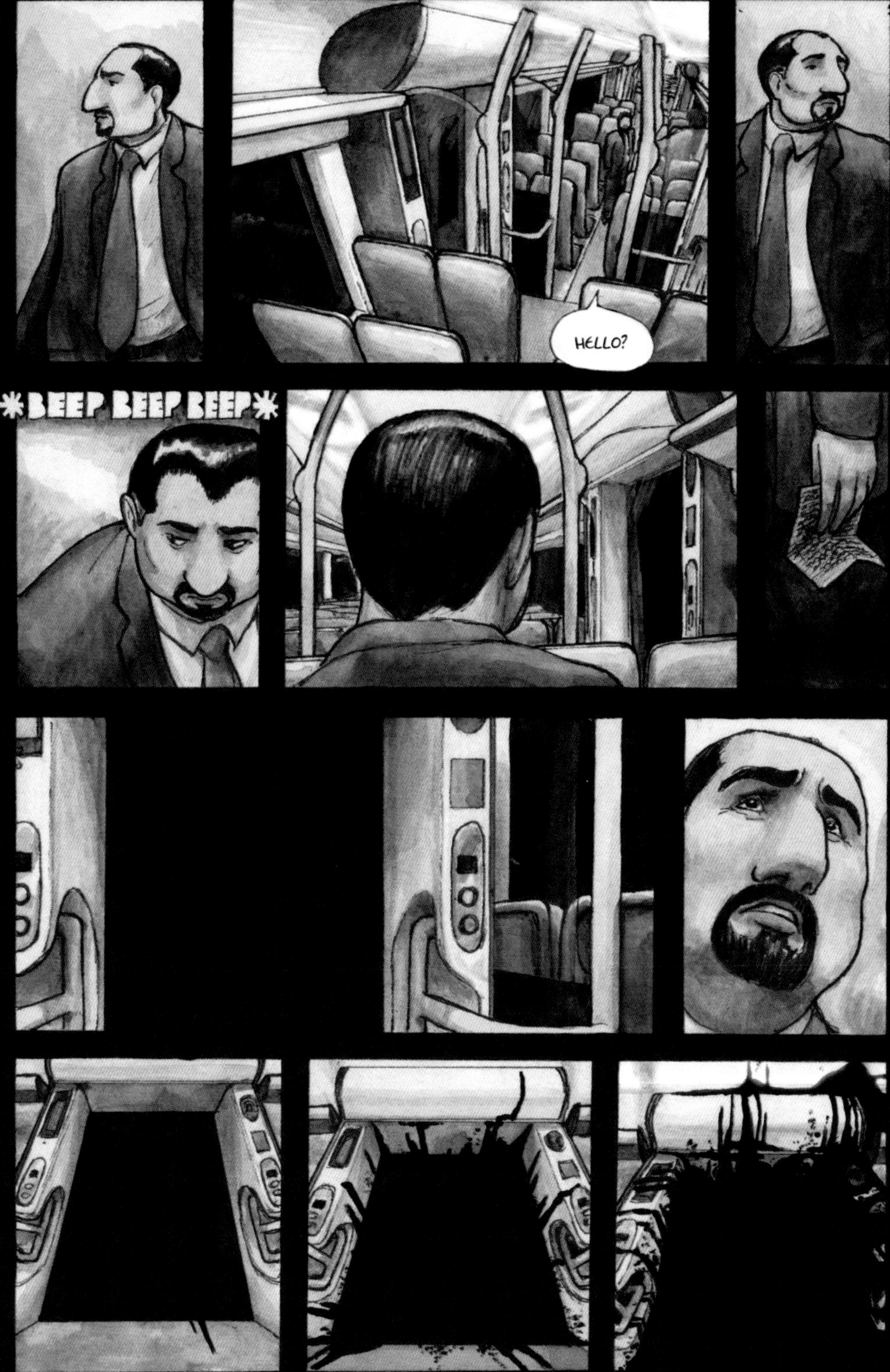
HELLO?
BEEP BEEP BEEP

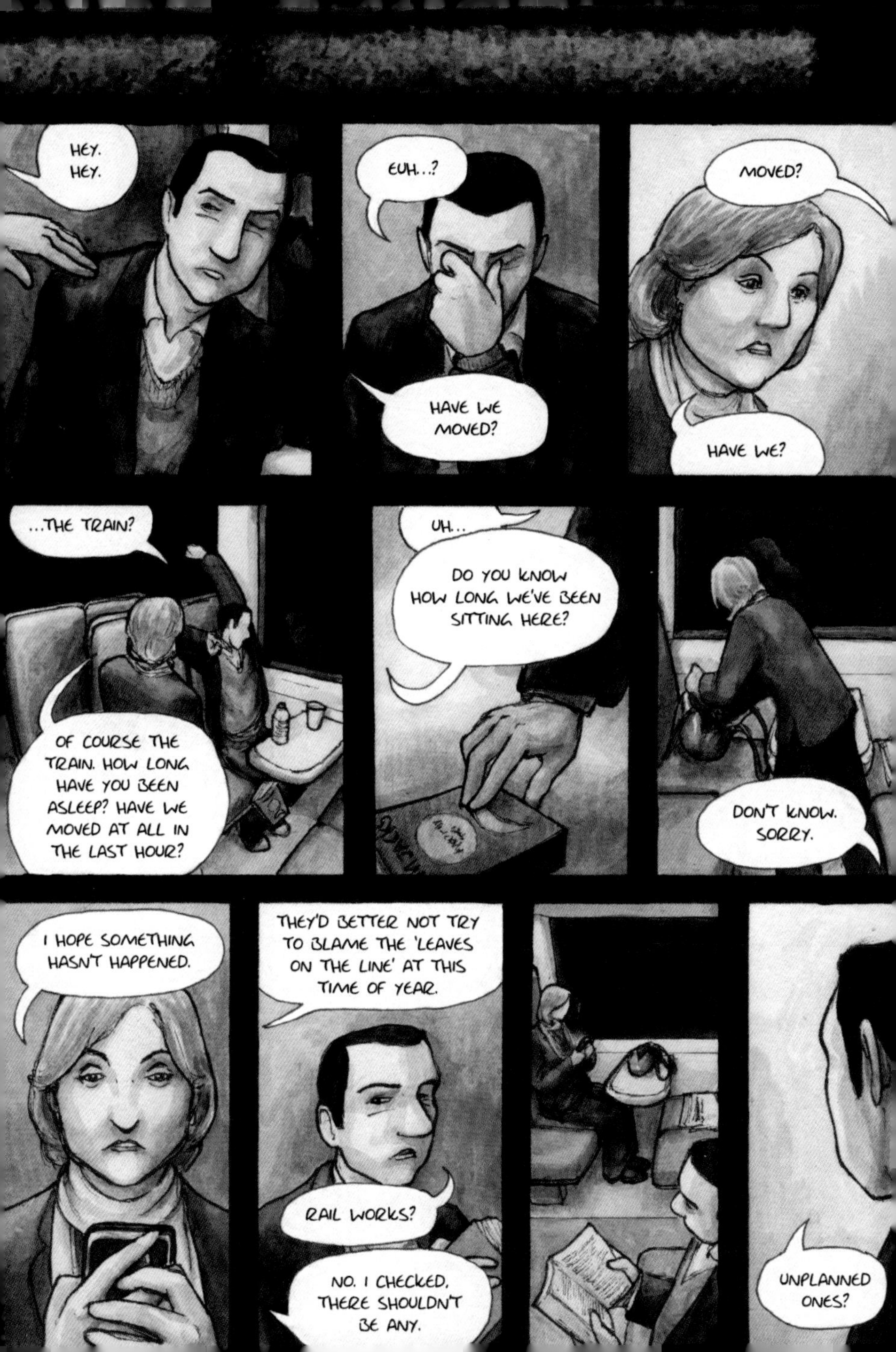
HEY.
HEY.
EUH...?
HAVE WE MOVED?
MOVED?
HAVE WE?
...THE TRAIN?
OF COURSE THE TRAIN. HOW LONG HAVE YOU BEEN ASLEEP? HAVE WE MOVED AT ALL IN THE LAST HOUR?
UH...
DO YOU KNOW HOW LONG WE'VE BEEN SITTING HERE?
DON'T KNOW. SORRY.
I HOPE SOMETHING HASN'T HAPPENED.
THEY'D BETTER NOT TRY TO BLAME THE 'LEAVES ON THE LINE' AT THIS TIME OF YEAR.
RAIL WORKS?
NO. I CHECKED, THERE SHOULDN'T BE ANY.
UNPLANNED ONES?

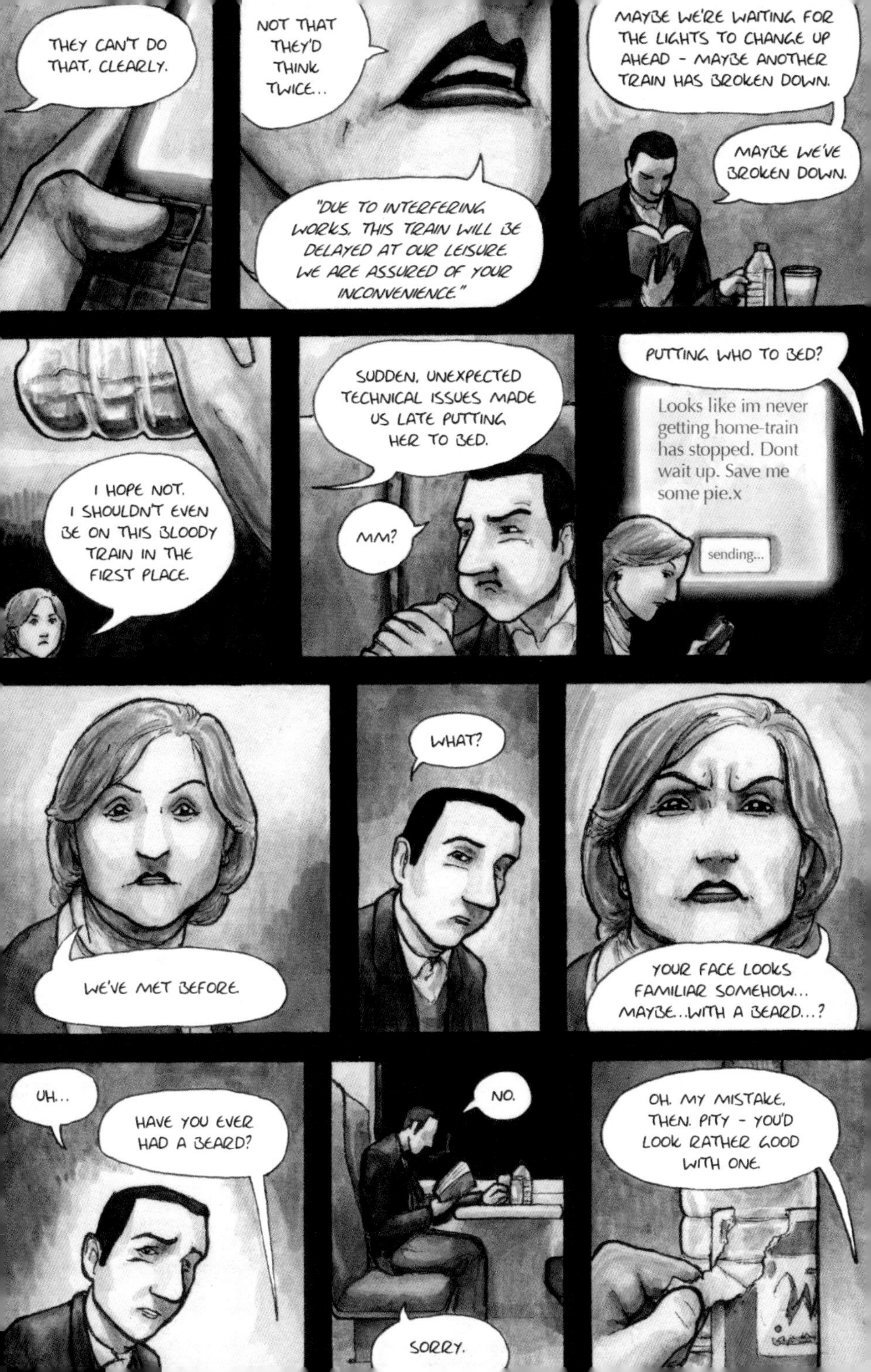
THEY CAN'T DO THAT, CLEARLY.
NOT THAT THEY'D THINK TWICE...
"DUE TO INTERFERING WORKS, THIS TRAIN WILL BE DELAYED AT OUR LEISURE. WE ARE ASSURED OF YOUR INCONVENIENCE."
MAYBE WE'RE WAITING FOR THE LIGHTS TO CHANGE UP AHEAD - MAYBE ANOTHER TRAIN HAS BROKEN DOWN.
MAYBE WE'VE BROKEN DOWN.
I HOPE NOT. I SHOULDN'T EVEN BE ON THIS BLOODY TRAIN IN THE FIRST PLACE.
SUDDEN, UNEXPECTED TECHNICAL ISSUES MADE US LATE PUTTING HER TO BED.
MM?
PUTTING WHO TO BED?
Looks like im never getting home-train has stopped. Dont wait up. Save me some pie.x
sending...
WE'VE MET BEFORE.
WHAT?
YOUR FACE LOOKS FAMILIAR SOMEHOW... MAYBE...WITH A BEARD...?
UH...
HAVE YOU EVER HAD A BEARD?
NO.
SORRY.
OH. MY MISTAKE, THEN. PITY - YOU'D LOOK RATHER GOOD WITH ONE.

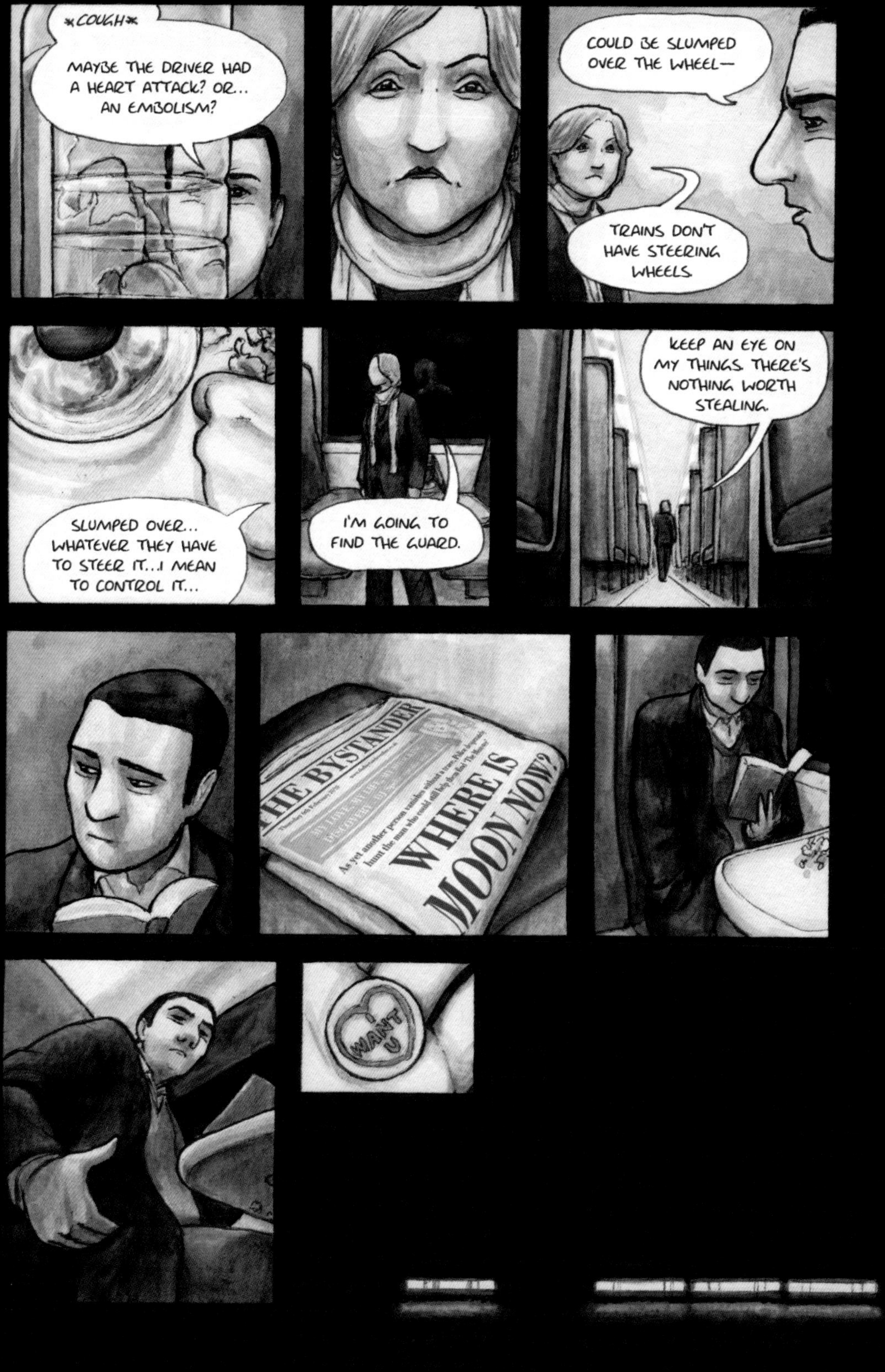
COUGH
MAYBE THE DRIVER HAD A HEART ATTACK? OR... AN EMBOLISM?
COULD BE SLUMPED OVER THE WHEEL—
TRAINS DON'T HAVE STEERING WHEELS.
SLUMPED OVER... WHATEVER THEY HAVE TO STEER IT...I MEAN TO CONTROL IT...
I'M GOING TO FIND THE GUARD.
KEEP AN EYE ON MY THINGS. THERE'S NOTHING WORTH STEALING.
THE BYSTANDER
WHERE IS MOON NOW?
WANT U

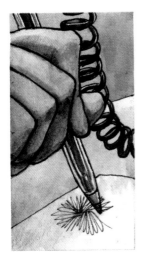

SORRY,
ARE YOU...?

DON'T WORRY:
TWELVE MINUTES ON
HOLD AND COUNTING!
WHAT CAN I DO
FOR YOU?

I JUST NEED YOU TO PUT
THIS APPLICATION THROUGH
AS A GREEN LIGHT...

COURSE.

WHAT?

YES...YES, HELLO,
I'M CALLING FROM THE
HARBANE TRUST, WE HELP TO
REINTEGRATE OFFENDERS
BACK INTO THE COMM—

...YES, I'LL HOLD.

EVERY TIME! I SHOULD PROBABLY HAVE TOLD THEM WE HELP THE 'FELONIOUSLY INCLINED'...OR 'PERSONS OF CONSEQUENTIALLY RESTRICTED LIBERTY'...

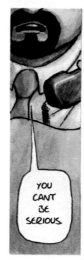

YOU CANT BE SERIOUS

I KNOW IT WAS REJECTED BEFORE, BUT THINGS HAVE CHANGED SOMEWHAT...

THIS IS THAT ABSURD REQUEST FOR MONEY FROM 'THE POSTMAN!'

PLEASE, WE'RE NOT A TABLOID RAG! RODNEY MOON.

DAVID, WE'VE ALREADY MADE OUR DECISION ON THIS...

BUT THAT DECISION WAS BASED ON THE SIZE OF THE REQUEST, AND IN LIGHT OF NEW CIRCUMSTANCES I THINK WE CAN OVERLOOK THAT.

WHAT NEW CIRCUMSTANCES?

IT WASN'T JUST BASED ON THE SIZE, IT WAS BASED ON HIS TECHNICALLY NOT BEING AN EX-OFFENDER FOLLOWING THE 'NOT GUILTY' VERDICT—

AND MORE IMPORTANTLY ON THE OUTCRY WE'D FACE FROM THE PUBLIC!

MOST PEOPLE STILL BELIEVE MOON IS 'THE FIEND', YOU KNOW!

YES?

SEBASTIAN—

DELVE. I KNOW.

MY REPUTATION PRECEDES ME...

SOMETHING LIKE THAT.

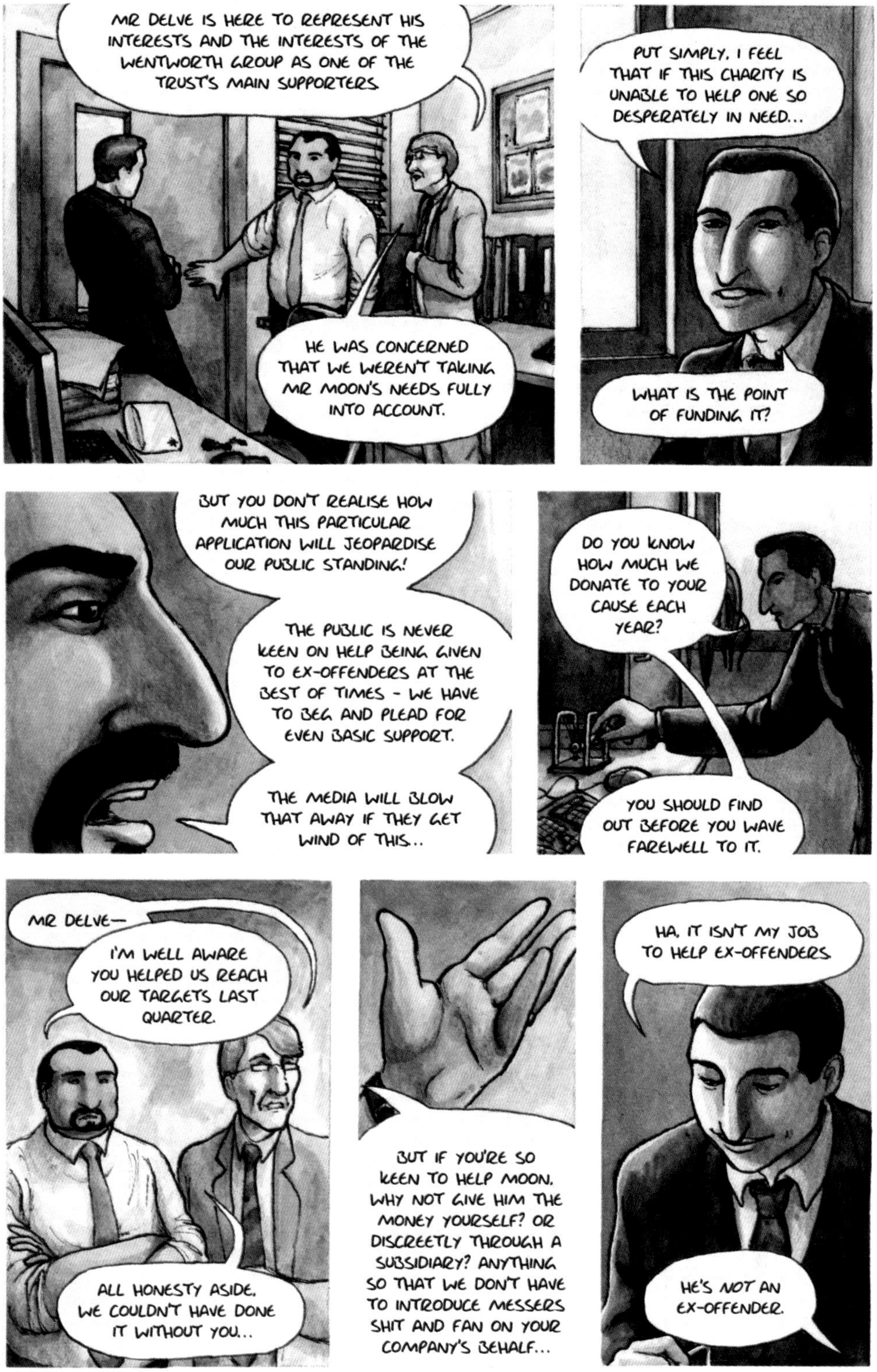
MR DELVE IS HERE TO REPRESENT HIS INTERESTS AND THE INTERESTS OF THE WENTWORTH GROUP AS ONE OF THE TRUST'S MAIN SUPPORTERS.
HE WAS CONCERNED THAT WE WEREN'T TAKING MR MOON'S NEEDS FULLY INTO ACCOUNT.
PUT SIMPLY, I FEEL THAT IF THIS CHARITY IS UNABLE TO HELP ONE SO DESPERATELY IN NEED...
WHAT IS THE POINT OF FUNDING IT?
BUT YOU DON'T REALISE HOW MUCH THIS PARTICULAR APPLICATION WILL JEOPARDISE OUR PUBLIC STANDING!
THE PUBLIC IS NEVER KEEN ON HELP BEING GIVEN TO EX-OFFENDERS AT THE BEST OF TIMES - WE HAVE TO BEG AND PLEAD FOR EVEN BASIC SUPPORT.
THE MEDIA WILL BLOW THAT AWAY IF THEY GET WIND OF THIS...
DO YOU KNOW HOW MUCH WE DONATE TO YOUR CAUSE EACH YEAR?
YOU SHOULD FIND OUT BEFORE YOU WAVE FAREWELL TO IT.
MR DELVE—
I'M WELL AWARE YOU HELPED US REACH OUR TARGETS LAST QUARTER.
ALL HONESTY ASIDE, WE COULDN'T HAVE DONE IT WITHOUT YOU...
BUT IF YOU'RE SO KEEN TO HELP MOON, WHY NOT GIVE HIM THE MONEY YOURSELF? OR DISCREETLY THROUGH A SUBSIDIARY? ANYTHING SO THAT WE DON'T HAVE TO INTRODUCE MESSERS SHIT AND FAN ON YOUR COMPANY'S BEHALF...
HA, IT ISN'T MY JOB TO HELP EX-OFFENDERS.
HE'S NOT AN EX-OFFENDER.

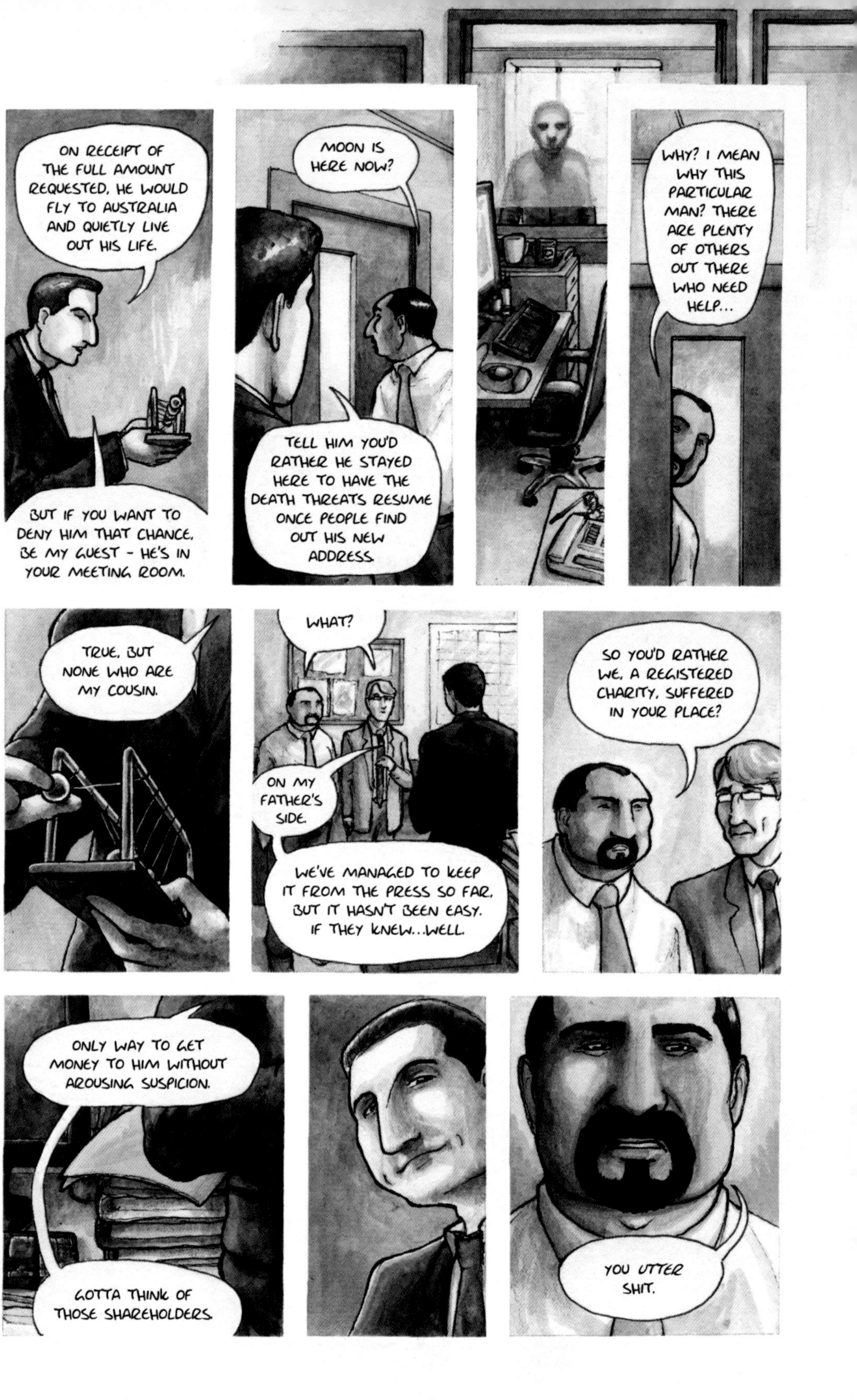
ON RECEIPT OF THE FULL AMOUNT REQUESTED, HE WOULD FLY TO AUSTRALIA AND QUIETLY LIVE OUT HIS LIFE.
BUT IF YOU WANT TO DENY HIM THAT CHANCE, BE MY GUEST - HE'S IN YOUR MEETING ROOM.
MOON IS HERE NOW?
TELL HIM YOU'D RATHER HE STAYED HERE TO HAVE THE DEATH THREATS RESUME ONCE PEOPLE FIND OUT HIS NEW ADDRESS.
WHY? I MEAN WHY THIS PARTICULAR MAN? THERE ARE PLENTY OF OTHERS OUT THERE WHO NEED HELP...
TRUE, BUT NONE WHO ARE MY COUSIN.
WHAT?
ON MY FATHER'S SIDE.
WE'VE MANAGED TO KEEP IT FROM THE PRESS SO FAR, BUT IT HASN'T BEEN EASY. IF THEY KNEW...WELL.
SO YOU'D RATHER WE, A REGISTERED CHARITY, SUFFERED IN YOUR PLACE?
ONLY WAY TO GET MONEY TO HIM WITHOUT AROUSING SUSPICION.
GOTTA THINK OF THOSE SHAREHOLDERS.
YOU UTTER SHIT.

HE'S NOT EXACTLY THE GODFEARING BENEVOLENT YOU TOLD ME HE WAS, IS HE?

ME DELVE, I DO APOLOGISE...MIGHT MY COLLEAGUE AND I JUST HAVE A QUICK CHAT? ALONE?

GO AHEAD. I'LL BE IN YOUR OFFICE.

SPLENDID.

DELVE ASIDE, WHY NOT THIS PARTICULAR MAN? NONE OF OUR APPLICANTS ARE EXACTLY...

SAINTS...

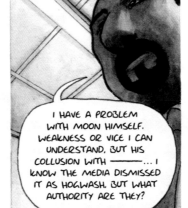

I HAVE A PROBLEM WITH MOON HIMSELF. WEAKNESS OR VICE I CAN UNDERSTAND, BUT HIS COLLUSION WITH ———... I KNOW THE MEDIA DISMISSED IT AS HOGWASH, BUT WHAT AUTHORITY ARE THEY?

OH COME NOW, YOU AREN'T TALKING ABOUT 'THE MONSTER' ACTUALLY BEING A MONSTER?

LOOK, I DON'T DOUBT THAT HE DIDN'T ABDUCT THOSE PEOPLE - THAT HE PASSED THEM THOSE LETTERS FROM THE REAL KIDNAPPER, NEVER KNOWING WHAT HAPPENED AFTERWARDS.

THE COURTS BELIEVED HIM; THEY JUST DIDN'T BELIEVE HIM WHEN HE SAID THEY WERE TAKEN BY SOMETHING OTHER THAN HUMAN...

BUT WHY DID HE DO IT AT ALL? THAT'S WHAT TROUBLES ME.

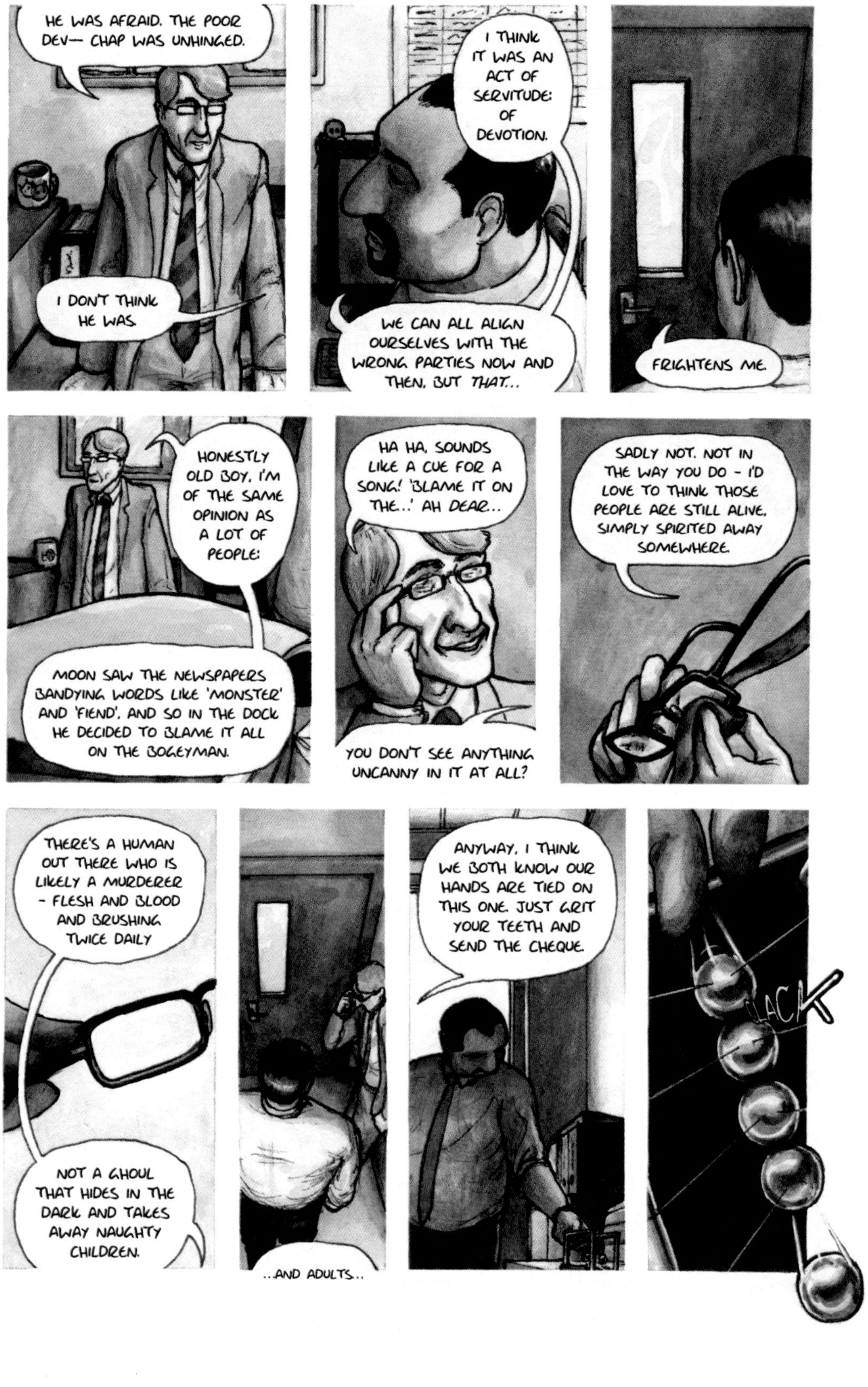
HE WAS AFRAID. THE POOR DEV— CHAP WAS UNHINGED.
I DON'T THINK HE WAS.
I THINK IT WAS AN ACT OF SERVITUDE: OF DEVOTION.
WE CAN ALL ALIGN OURSELVES WITH THE WRONG PARTIES NOW AND THEN, BUT THAT...
FRIGHTENS ME.
HONESTLY OLD BOY, I'M OF THE SAME OPINION AS A LOT OF PEOPLE:
MOON SAW THE NEWSPAPERS BANDYING WORDS LIKE 'MONSTER' AND 'FIEND', AND SO IN THE DOCK HE DECIDED TO BLAME IT ALL ON THE BOGEYMAN.
HA HA, SOUNDS LIKE A CUE FOR A SONG! 'BLAME IT ON THE...' AH DEAR...
YOU DON'T SEE ANYTHING UNCANNY IN IT AT ALL?
SADLY NOT. NOT IN THE WAY YOU DO - I'D LOVE TO THINK THOSE PEOPLE ARE STILL ALIVE, SIMPLY SPIRITED AWAY SOMEWHERE.
THERE'S A HUMAN OUT THERE WHO IS LIKELY A MURDERER - FLESH AND BLOOD AND BRUSHING TWICE DAILY
NOT A GHOUL THAT HIDES IN THE DARK AND TAKES AWAY NAUGHTY CHILDREN.
...AND ADULTS...
ANYWAY, I THINK WE BOTH KNOW OUR HANDS ARE TIED ON THIS ONE. JUST GRIT YOUR TEETH AND SEND THE CHEQUE.
CLACK

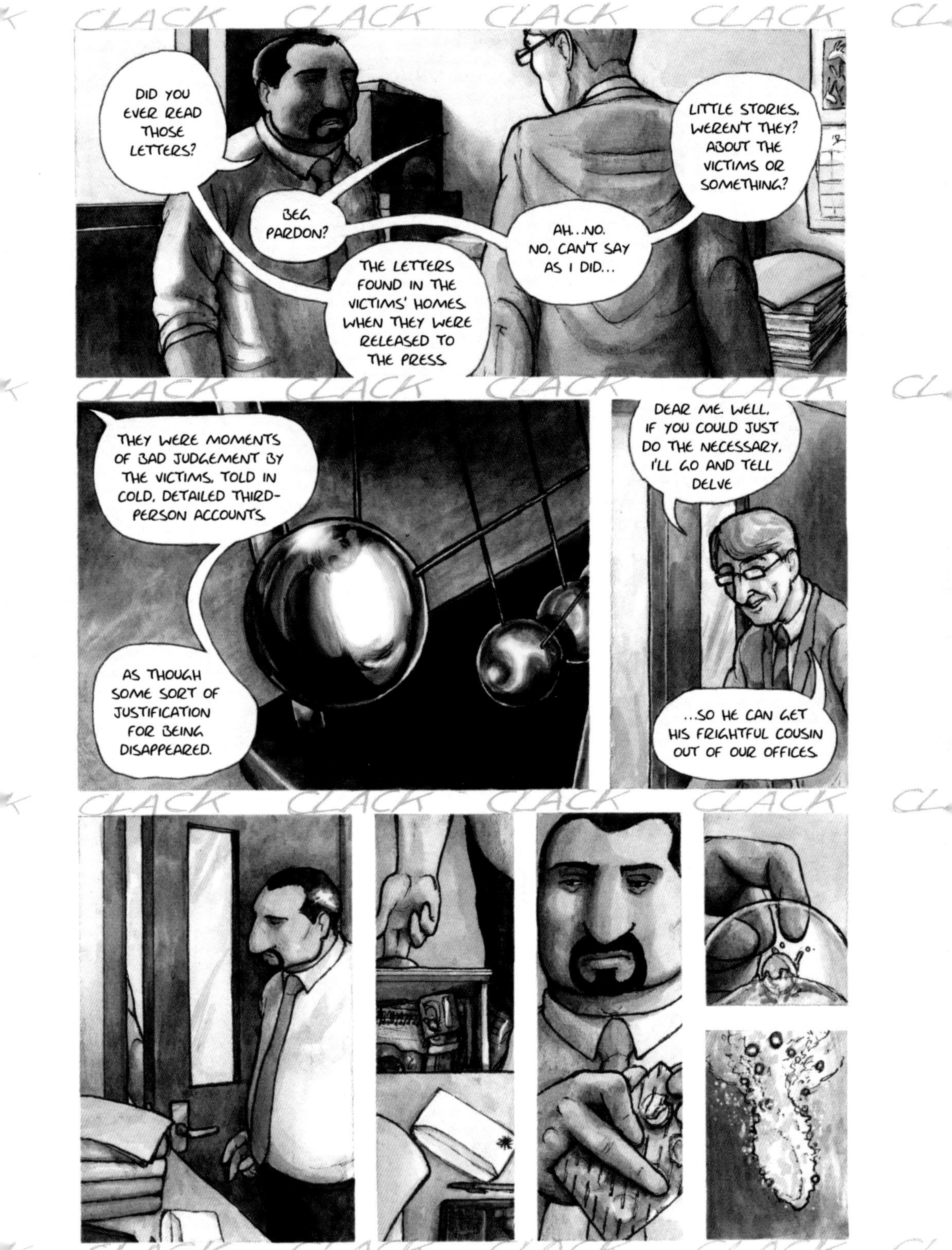

CLACK CLACK CLACK CLACK
DID YOU EVER READ THOSE LETTERS?
BEG PARDON?
THE LETTERS FOUND IN THE VICTIMS' HOMES. WHEN THEY WERE RELEASED TO THE PRESS.
AH...NO. NO, CAN'T SAY AS I DID...
LITTLE STORIES, WEREN'T THEY? ABOUT THE VICTIMS OR SOMETHING?
CLACK CLACK CLACK CLACK
THEY WERE MOMENTS OF BAD JUDGEMENT BY THE VICTIMS, TOLD IN COLD, DETAILED THIRD-PERSON ACCOUNTS.
AS THOUGH SOME SORT OF JUSTIFICATION FOR BEING DISAPPEARED.
DEAR ME. WELL, IF YOU COULD JUST DO THE NECESSARY, I'LL GO AND TELL DELVE
...SO HE CAN GET HIS FRIGHTFUL COUSIN OUT OF OUR OFFICES.
CLACK CLACK CLACK CLACK
CLACK CLACK CLACK CLACK

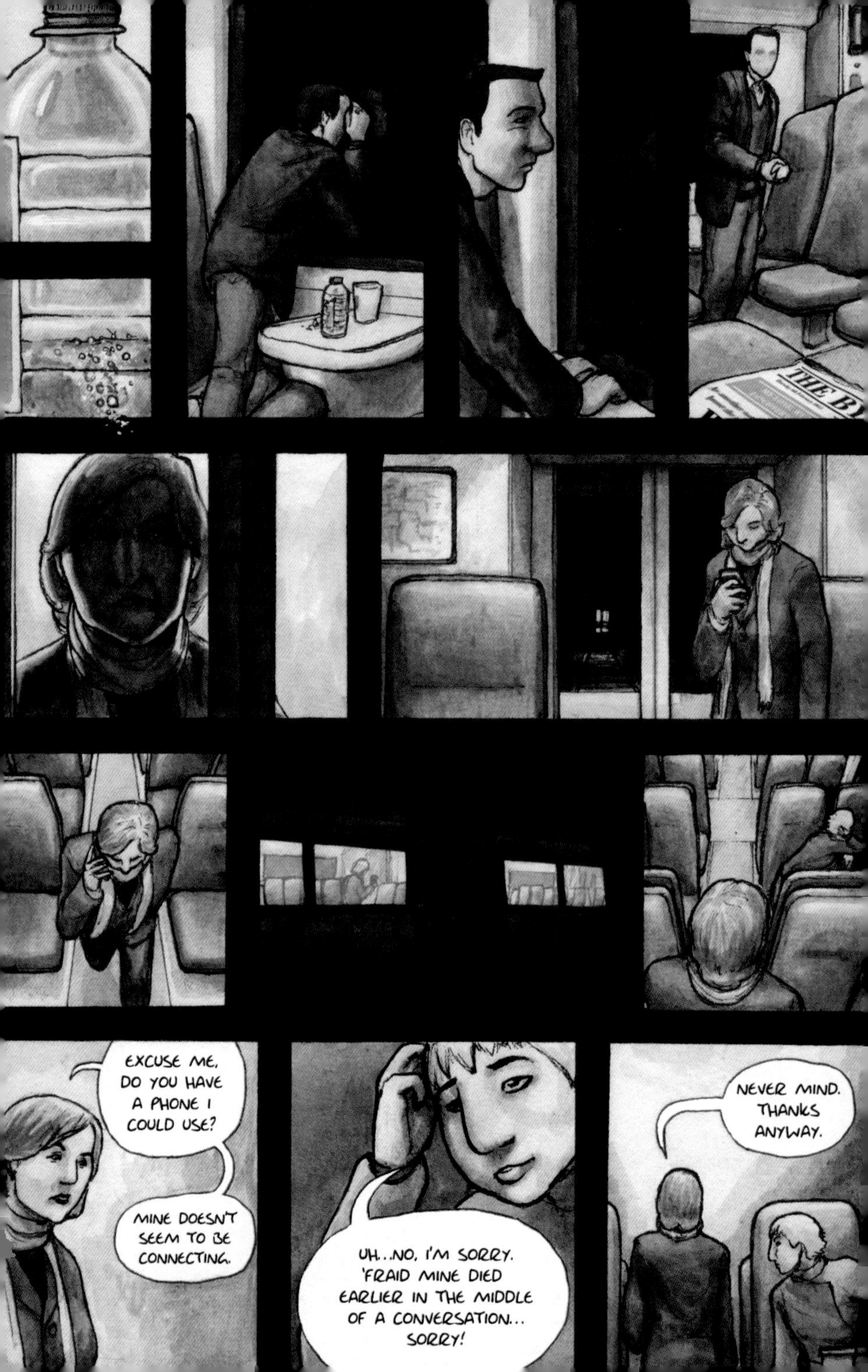

THE B
EXCUSE ME, DO YOU HAVE A PHONE I COULD USE?
MINE DOESN'T SEEM TO BE CONNECTING.
UH...NO, I'M SORRY. 'FRAID MINE DIED EARLIER IN THE MIDDLE OF A CONVERSATION... SORRY!
NEVER MIND. THANKS ANYWAY.

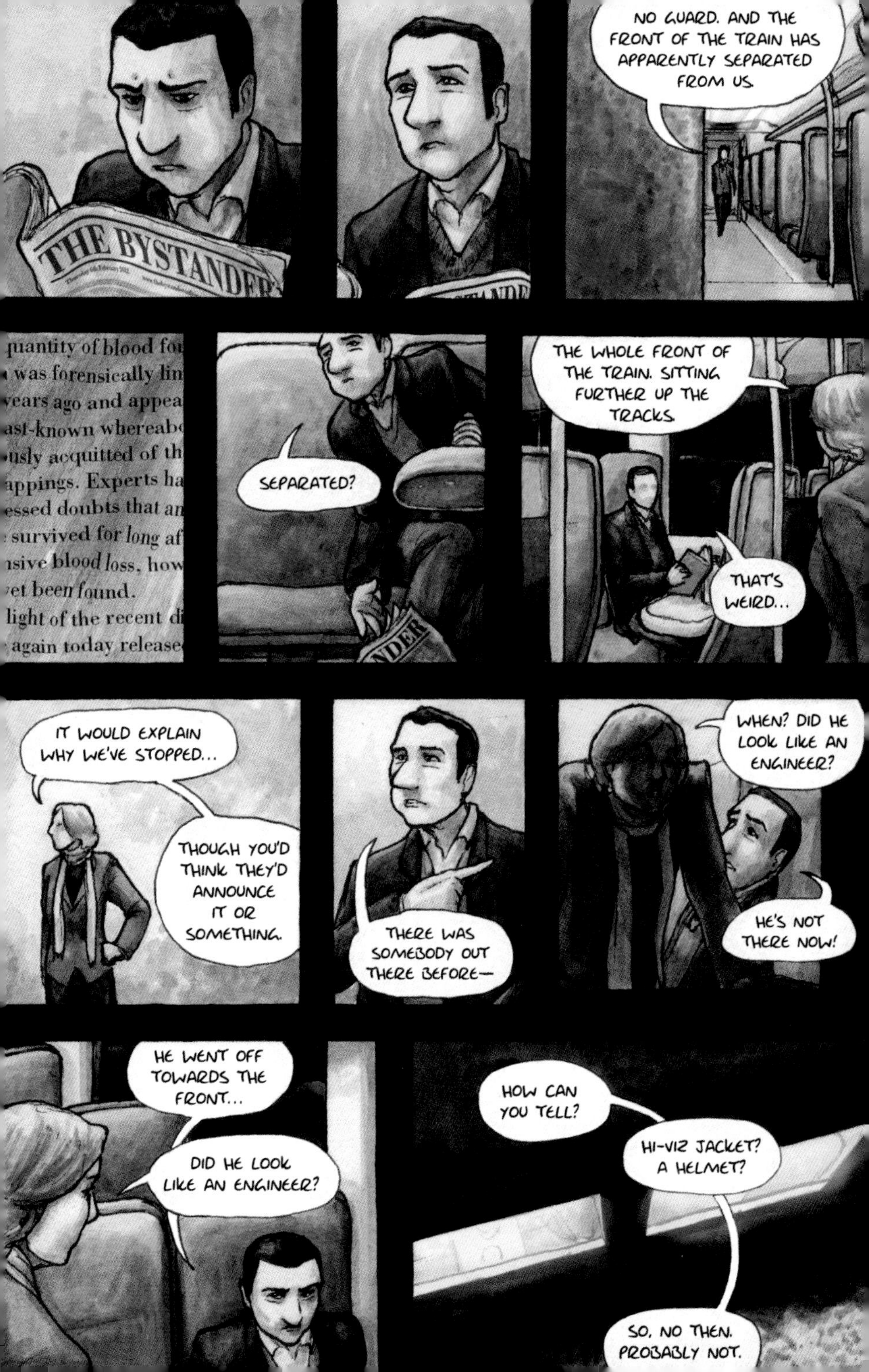
THE BYSTANDER
NO GUARD. AND THE FRONT OF THE TRAIN HAS APPARENTLY SEPARATED FROM US.
quantity of blood fo
was forensically lin
years ago and appea
ast-known whereab
usly acquitted of th
appings. Experts ha
essed doubts that an
survived for long af
nsive blood loss, how
et been found.
light of the recent d
again today release
SEPARATED?
THE WHOLE FRONT OF THE TRAIN. SITTING FURTHER UP THE TRACKS.
THAT'S WEIRD...
IT WOULD EXPLAIN WHY WE'VE STOPPED...
THOUGH YOU'D THINK THEY'D ANNOUNCE IT OR SOMETHING.
THERE WAS SOMEBODY OUT THERE BEFORE—
WHEN? DID HE LOOK LIKE AN ENGINEER?
HE'S NOT THERE NOW!
HE WENT OFF TOWARDS THE FRONT...
DID HE LOOK LIKE AN ENGINEER?
HOW CAN YOU TELL?
HI-VIZ JACKET? A HELMET?
SO, NO THEN. PROBABLY NOT.

DO YOU HAVE A PHONE? IS IT WORKING?

NO.

DON'T TELL ME IT'S NOT WORKING EITHER?

DON'T HAVE ONE. I DON'T LIKE MOBILES

OH, I SEE. A GENTLEMAN OF THE BACKWARDIAN ERA

JUST DON'T LIKE TO BE BOTHERED BY PEOPLE. THAT'S ALL.

RATHER BE LEFT ALONE.

WELL WE CERTAINLY ARE THAT, NOW. ALL ALONE.

AHA!

J·M JACKS

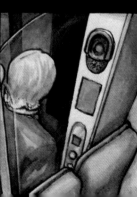

ARE YOU ALLOWED TO USE THAT?

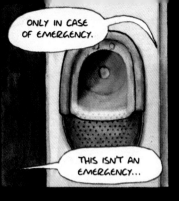

ONLY IN CASE OF EMERGENCY.

THIS ISN'T AN EMERGENCY...

HOW DO YOU KNOW?

Push button

Wait for response

Speak to driver

Penalty for improper use

I'M STAYING OUT OF IT.

IT'S JUST FOR TALKING TO THE DRIVER!

I DON'T CARE. PEOPLE SEE YOU NEAR IT, YOU'RE AUTOMATICALLY INVOLVED.

WHAT PEOPLE?

CCTV? GOD, THE PARANOIA...!

WHAT DOES 'IMPROPER USE' MEAN, ANYWAY?

CLEARLY THAT'S A TERM OPEN TO ABUSE.

'LOVE HEARTS'?
CAN I HAVE ONE?

KISS ME

BACK
OFF!!

PARDON?

LOOK, I JUST DON'T GO
FOR THE OLDER LADY!

"OLDER..."?

SO STOP STARING
AT ME AND DON'T...
DON'T *TOUCH* ME OR PRETEND
YOU *RECOGNISE* ME BECAUSE
YOU DEFINITELY DON'T—

I WAS READING
THE SWEET.

...OH...

RECOGNISING
YOUR FACE
IS NOT A
CODED
REQUEST TO
SEE YOUR
LITTLE WINKIE.

SORRY, UH... I THINK I
MUST'VE GOTTEN THE WRONG
END OF THE STICK...

CLEARLY YOU'VE
GOT THE WRONG
FUCKING TREE.

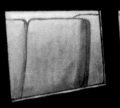

CRYPTIC OR NORMAL?

ALREADY DONE THE CRYPTIC.

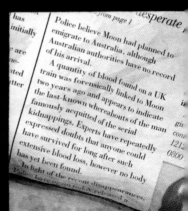

from page 1
...desperate

...has
...initially
...e are
...ne-
...ited
...tter

Police believe Moon had planned to emigrate to Australia, although Australian authorities have no record of his arrival.

A quantity of blood found on a UK train was forensically linked to Moon two years ago and appears to indicate the last-known whereabouts of the man famously acquitted of the serial kidnappings. Experts have repeatedly expressed doubts that anyone could have survived for long after such extensive blood loss, however no body has yet been found.

In light of the recent disappearances...

1212
0800

THIRTEEN-LETTER WORD MEANING 'UNCOMPROMISINGLY JUST'.

THIRTEEN?

R, H, SOMETHING, SOMETHING, SOMETHING, SOMETHING, A, N, SOMETHING, H, SOMETHING, SOMETHING, SOMETHING.

...RIGHTEOUS?

I'M GOING TO PUSH THE BUTTON.

HELLO?

HELLO? FABULOUS! CAN YOU TELL US WHY WE'VE STOPPED?

HELLO?

SORRY?

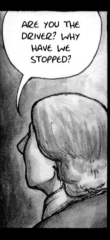

ARE YOU THE DRIVER? WHY HAVE WE STOPPED?

HEAR

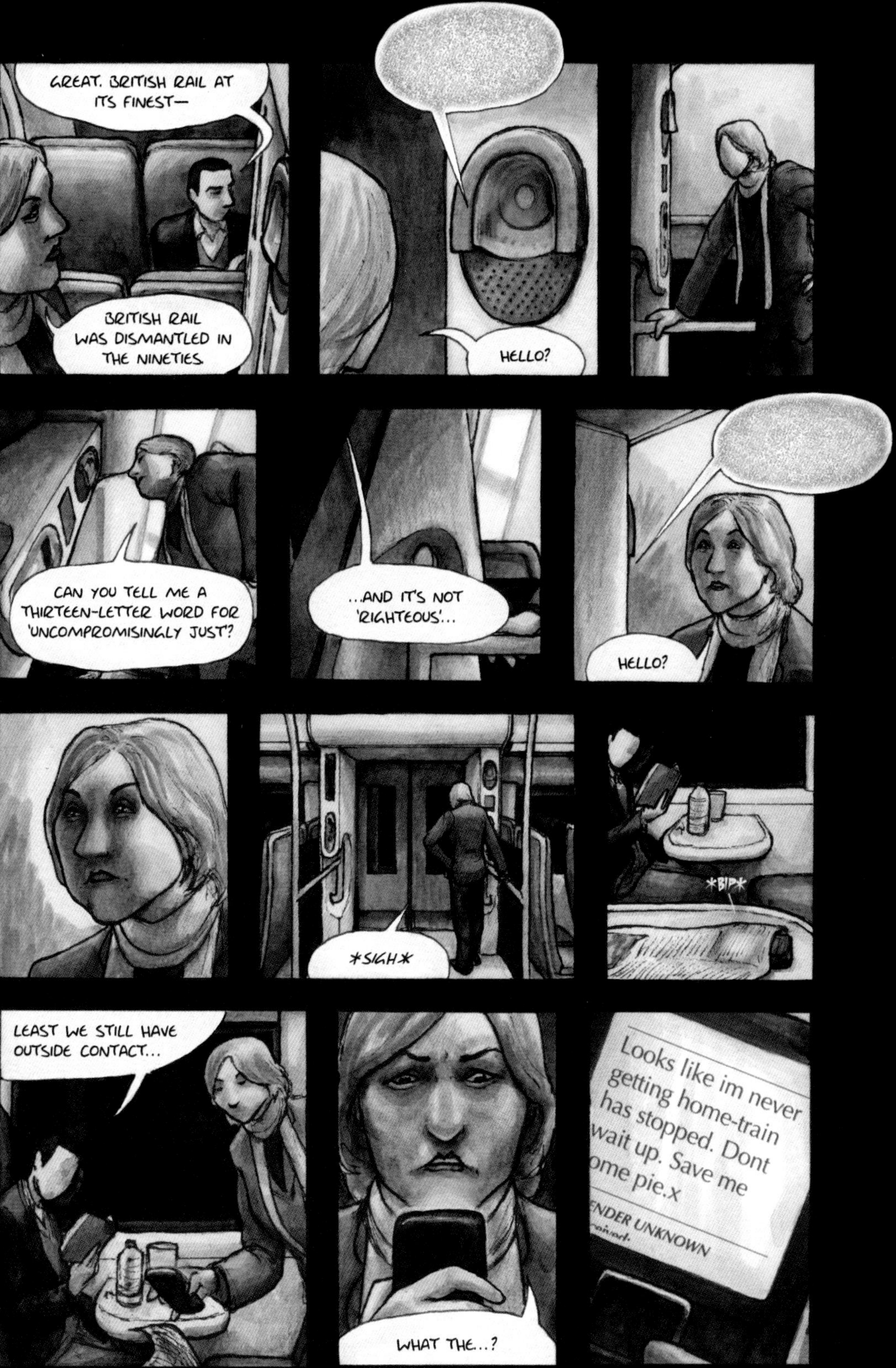
GREAT. BRITISH RAIL AT ITS FINEST—
BRITISH RAIL WAS DISMANTLED IN THE NINETIES.
HELLO?
CAN YOU TELL ME A THIRTEEN-LETTER WORD FOR 'UNCOMPROMISINGLY JUST'?
...AND IT'S NOT 'RIGHTEOUS'...
HELLO?
SIGH
BIP
LEAST WE STILL HAVE OUTSIDE CONTACT...
WHAT THE...?
Looks like im never
getting home-train
has stopped. Dont
wait up. Save me
ome pie.x
ENDER UNKNOWN

WHAT? IS IT WORKING OR NOT?

THIS ALL FEELS LIKE ONE BIG, ELABORATE JOKE.

ONE WE'RE NOT IN ON—

...OH GOD...

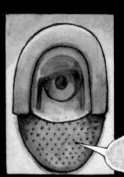

THIS CAN'T BE

OH GOD

OH GOD
NO

...WHAT...?

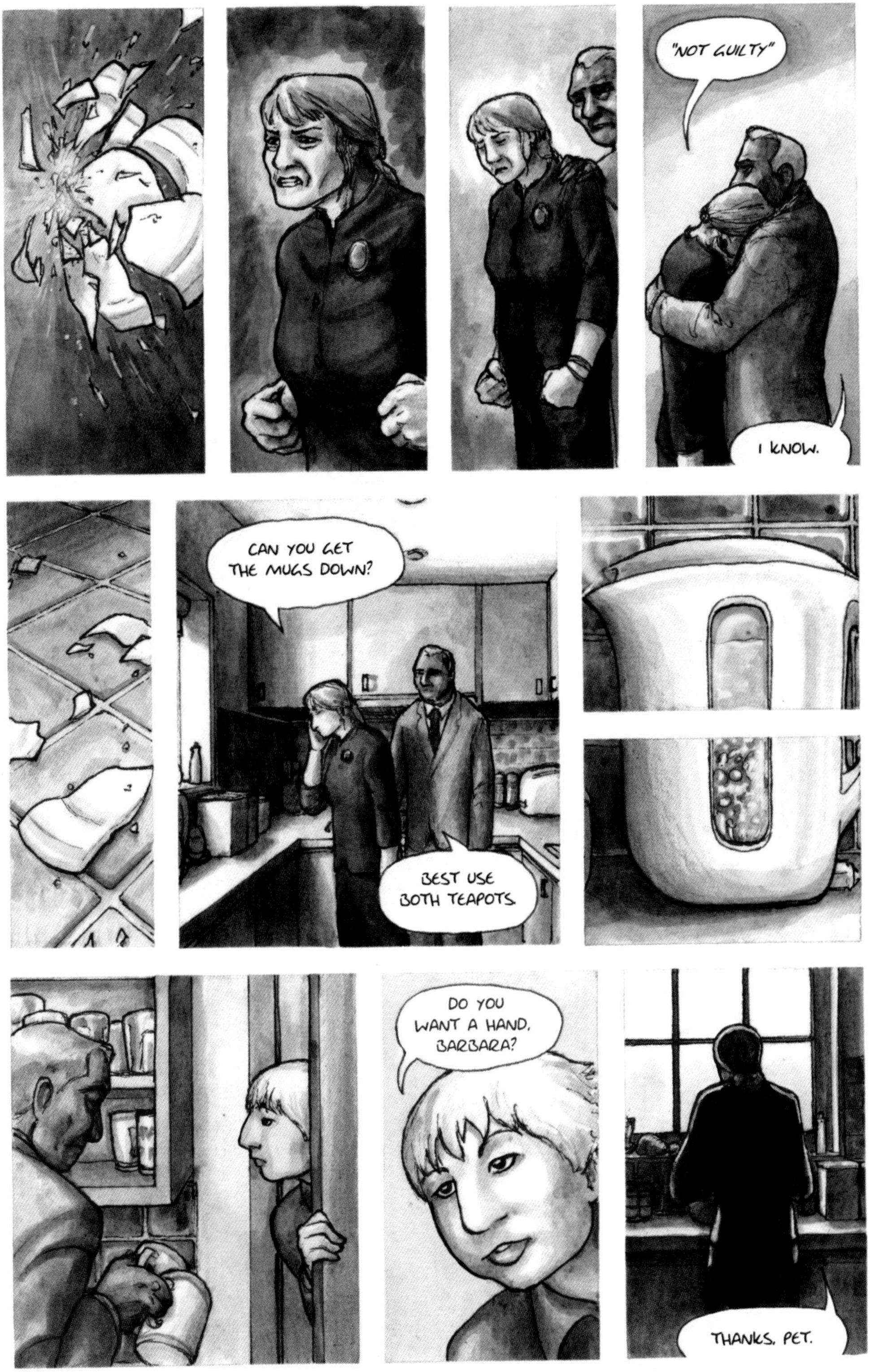
"NOT GUILTY"
I KNOW.
CAN YOU GET THE MUGS DOWN?
BEST USE BOTH TEAPOTS.
DO YOU WANT A HAND, BARBARA?
THANKS, PET.

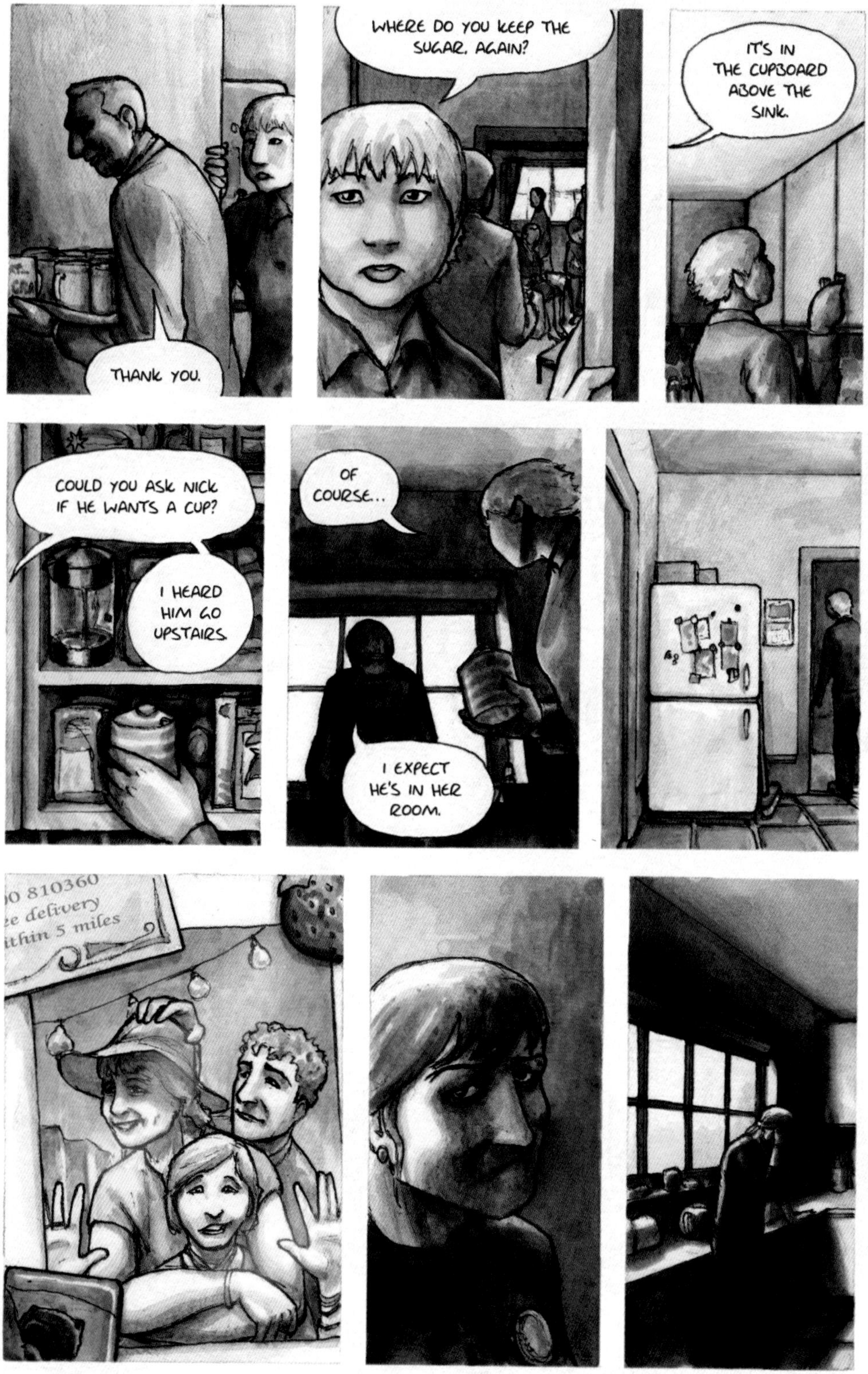
THANK YOU.
WHERE DO YOU KEEP THE SUGAR, AGAIN?
IT'S IN THE CUPBOARD ABOVE THE SINK.
COULD YOU ASK NICK IF HE WANTS A CUP?
I HEARD HIM GO UPSTAIRS.
OF COURSE...
I EXPECT HE'S IN HER ROOM.
0 810360
e delivery
ithin 5 miles

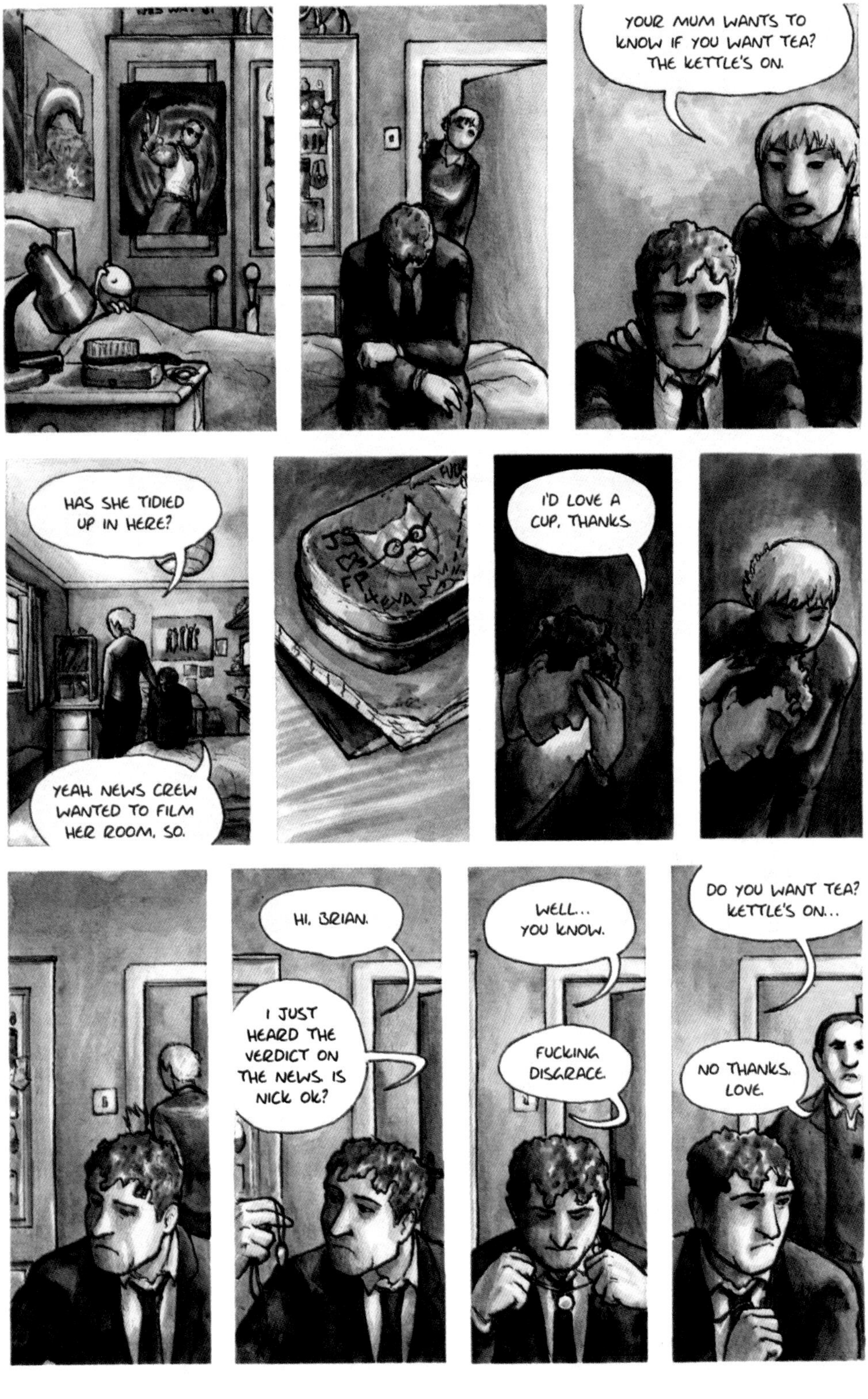
YOUR MUM WANTS TO KNOW IF YOU WANT TEA? THE KETTLE'S ON.
HAS SHE TIDIED UP IN HERE?
YEAH. NEWS CREW WANTED TO FILM HER ROOM, SO.
I'D LOVE A CUP, THANKS.
HI, BRIAN.
I JUST HEARD THE VERDICT ON THE NEWS. IS NICK OK?
WELL... YOU KNOW.
FUCKING DISGRACE.
DO YOU WANT TEA? KETTLE'S ON...
NO THANKS, LOVE.

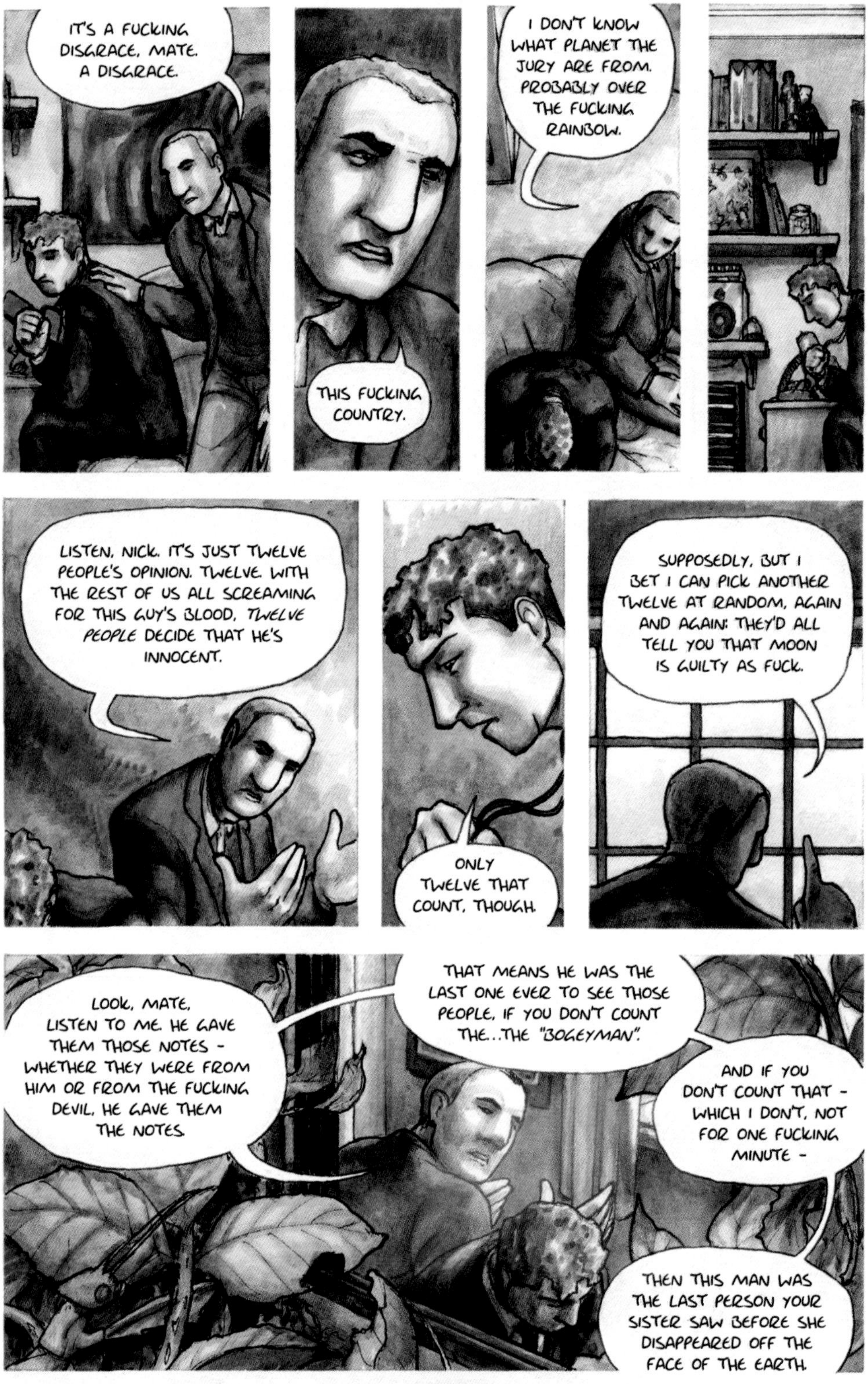
IT'S A FUCKING DISGRACE, MATE. A DISGRACE.
THIS FUCKING COUNTRY.
I DON'T KNOW WHAT PLANET THE JURY ARE FROM. PROBABLY OVER THE FUCKING RAINBOW.
LISTEN, NICK. IT'S JUST TWELVE PEOPLE'S OPINION. TWELVE. WITH THE REST OF US ALL SCREAMING FOR THIS GUY'S BLOOD, *TWELVE PEOPLE* DECIDE THAT HE'S INNOCENT.
ONLY TWELVE THAT COUNT, THOUGH.
SUPPOSEDLY, BUT I BET I CAN PICK ANOTHER TWELVE AT RANDOM, AGAIN AND AGAIN: THEY'D ALL TELL YOU THAT MOON IS GUILTY AS FUCK.
LOOK, MATE, LISTEN TO ME. HE GAVE THEM THOSE NOTES - WHETHER THEY WERE FROM HIM OR FROM THE FUCKING DEVIL, HE GAVE THEM THE NOTES.
THAT MEANS HE WAS THE LAST ONE EVER TO SEE THOSE PEOPLE, IF YOU DON'T COUNT THE... THE *"BOGEYMAN"*.
AND IF YOU DON'T COUNT THAT - WHICH I DON'T, NOT FOR ONE FUCKING MINUTE -
THEN THIS MAN WAS THE LAST PERSON YOUR SISTER SAW BEFORE SHE DISAPPEARED OFF THE FACE OF THE EARTH.

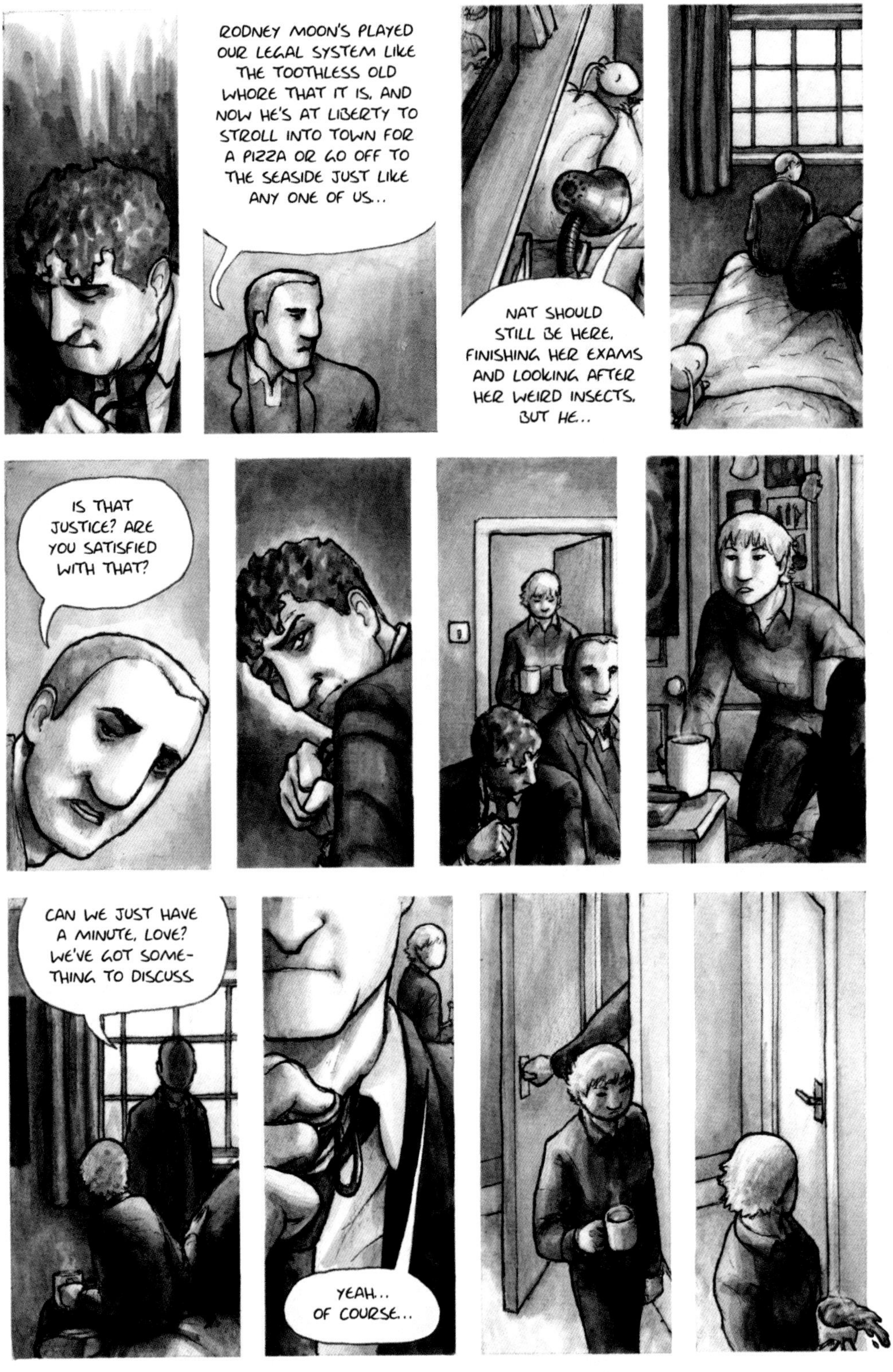
RODNEY MOON'S PLAYED OUR LEGAL SYSTEM LIKE THE TOOTHLESS OLD WHORE THAT IT IS, AND NOW HE'S AT LIBERTY TO STROLL INTO TOWN FOR A PIZZA OR GO OFF TO THE SEASIDE JUST LIKE ANY ONE OF US..
NAT SHOULD STILL BE HERE, FINISHING HER EXAMS AND LOOKING AFTER HER WEIRD INSECTS. BUT HE..
IS THAT JUSTICE? ARE YOU SATISFIED WITH THAT?
CAN WE JUST HAVE A MINUTE, LOVE? WE'VE GOT SOME-THING TO DISCUSS.
YEAH.. OF COURSE..

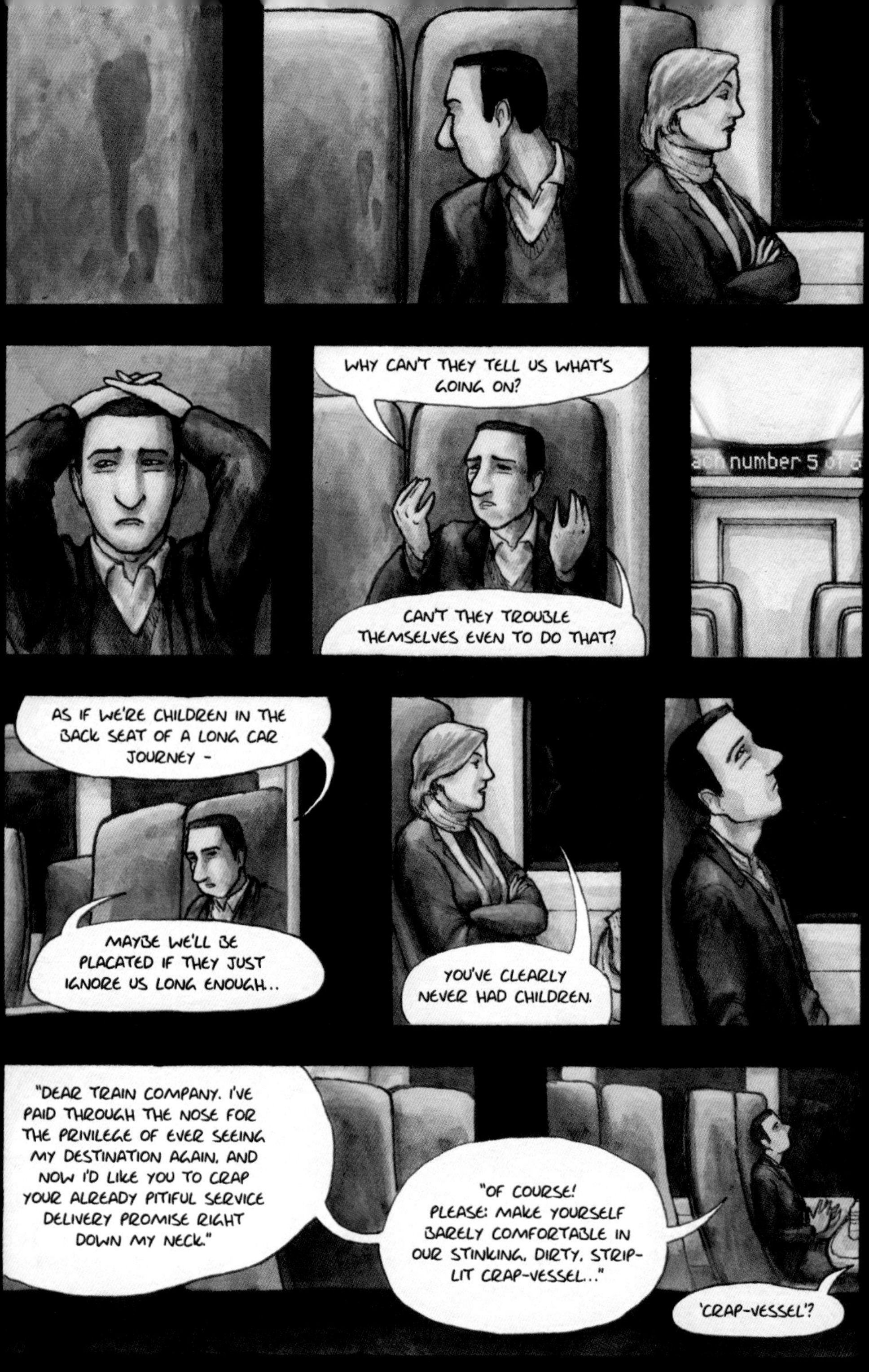
number 5 of
WHY CAN'T THEY TELL US WHAT'S GOING ON?
CAN'T THEY TROUBLE THEMSELVES EVEN TO DO THAT?
AS IF WE'RE CHILDREN IN THE BACK SEAT OF A LONG CAR JOURNEY -
MAYBE WE'LL BE PLACATED IF THEY JUST IGNORE US LONG ENOUGH...
YOU'VE CLEARLY NEVER HAD CHILDREN.
"DEAR TRAIN COMPANY. I'VE PAID THROUGH THE NOSE FOR THE PRIVILEGE OF EVER SEEING MY DESTINATION AGAIN, AND NOW I'D LIKE YOU TO CRAP YOUR ALREADY PITIFUL SERVICE DELIVERY PROMISE RIGHT DOWN MY NECK."
"OF COURSE! PLEASE: MAKE YOURSELF BARELY COMFORTABLE IN OUR STINKING, DIRTY, STRIP-LIT CRAP-VESSEL..."
'CRAP-VESSEL'?

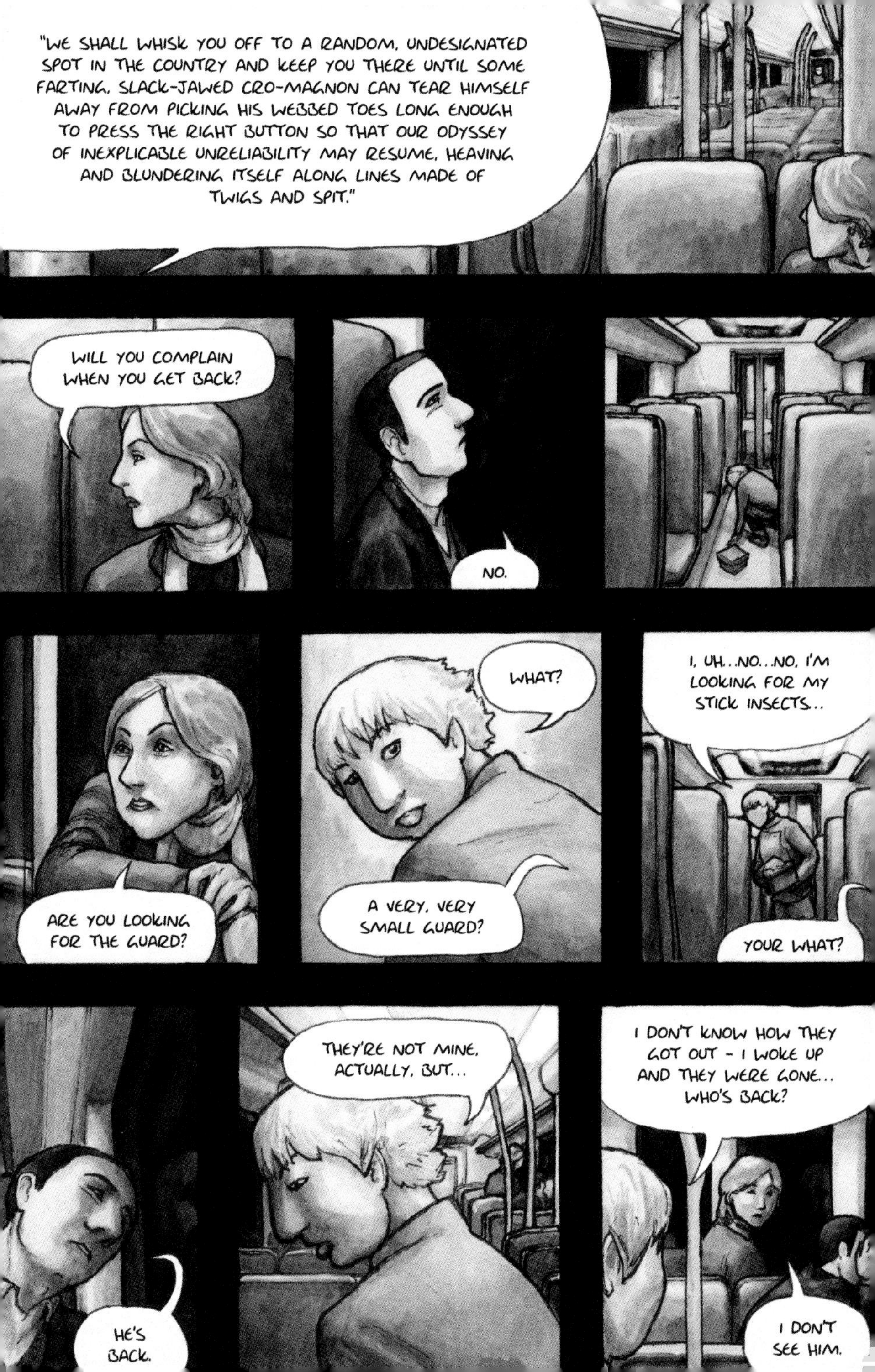
"WE SHALL WHISK YOU OFF TO A RANDOM, UNDESIGNATED SPOT IN THE COUNTRY AND KEEP YOU THERE UNTIL SOME FARTING, SLACK-JAWED CRO-MAGNON CAN TEAR HIMSELF AWAY FROM PICKING HIS WEBBED TOES LONG ENOUGH TO PRESS THE RIGHT BUTTON SO THAT OUR ODYSSEY OF INEXPLICABLE UNRELIABILITY MAY RESUME, HEAVING AND BLUNDERING ITSELF ALONG LINES MADE OF TWIGS AND SPIT."
WILL YOU COMPLAIN WHEN YOU GET BACK?
NO.
ARE YOU LOOKING FOR THE GUARD?
WHAT?
A VERY, VERY SMALL GUARD?
I, UH...NO...NO, I'M LOOKING FOR MY STICK INSECTS...
YOUR WHAT?
HE'S BACK.
THEY'RE NOT MINE, ACTUALLY, BUT...
I DON'T KNOW HOW THEY GOT OUT - I WOKE UP AND THEY WERE GONE... WHO'S BACK?
I DON'T SEE HIM.

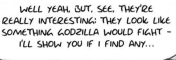

HE WAS RIGHT THERE...

STICK INSECTS? YOU'RE LOOKING FOR STICK INSECTS?

WELL YEAH, BUT, SEE, THEY'RE REALLY INTERESTING; THEY LOOK LIKE SOMETHING GODZILLA WOULD FIGHT - I'LL SHOW YOU IF I FIND ANY...

ARE THEY POISONOUS?

NO, NO. I MEAN, THEY SPRAY A KIND OF FOUL-SMELLING LIQUID IF YOU THREATEN THEM

FOUL-SMELLING?!

IT'S HARMLESS...

MY GOD, THAT'S VILE.

ARE THEY EXOTIC?

QUITE EXOTIC, I GUESS.

THEN SOMEBODY STOLE THEM.

BUT, WAIT, THE BOX WAS UNDER MY ARMS - I'M SURE I WOULD'VE NOTICED ANYONE MOVING IT...

CLEARLY NOT. EVIDENTLY THEY GOT OFF THE TRAIN WITH EVERYONE ELSE.

...NICK'S GOING TO KILL ME...

WHILE LOOKING FOR BUGS, YOU DIDN'T HAPPEN TO SEE THE GUARD, DID YOU?

NO, SORRY. I HAVEN'T SEEN ANYONE AT ALL, ACTUALLY...

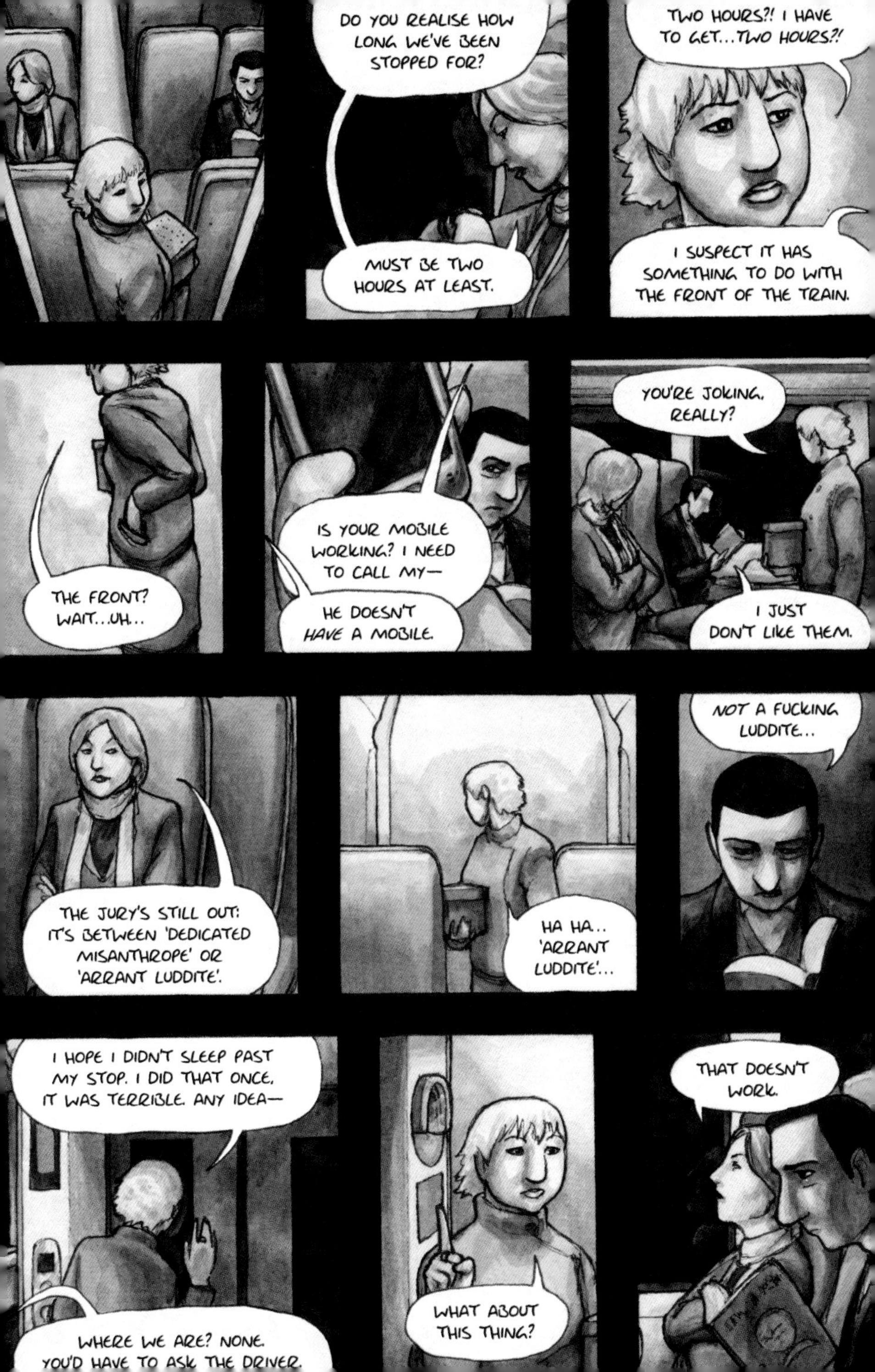
DO YOU REALISE HOW LONG WE'VE BEEN STOPPED FOR?
MUST BE TWO HOURS AT LEAST.
TWO HOURS?! I HAVE TO GET... TWO HOURS?!
I SUSPECT IT HAS SOMETHING TO DO WITH THE FRONT OF THE TRAIN.
THE FRONT? WAIT... UH...
IS YOUR MOBILE WORKING? I NEED TO CALL MY—
HE DOESN'T HAVE A MOBILE.
YOU'RE JOKING. REALLY?
I JUST DON'T LIKE THEM.
THE JURY'S STILL OUT: IT'S BETWEEN 'DEDICATED MISANTHROPE' OR 'ARRANT LUDDITE'.
HA HA.. 'ARRANT LUDDITE'...
NOT A FUCKING LUDDITE...
I HOPE I DIDN'T SLEEP PAST MY STOP. I DID THAT ONCE. IT WAS TERRIBLE. ANY IDEA—
WHERE WE ARE? NONE. YOU'D HAVE TO ASK THE DRIVER.
WHAT ABOUT THIS THING?
THAT DOESN'T WORK.

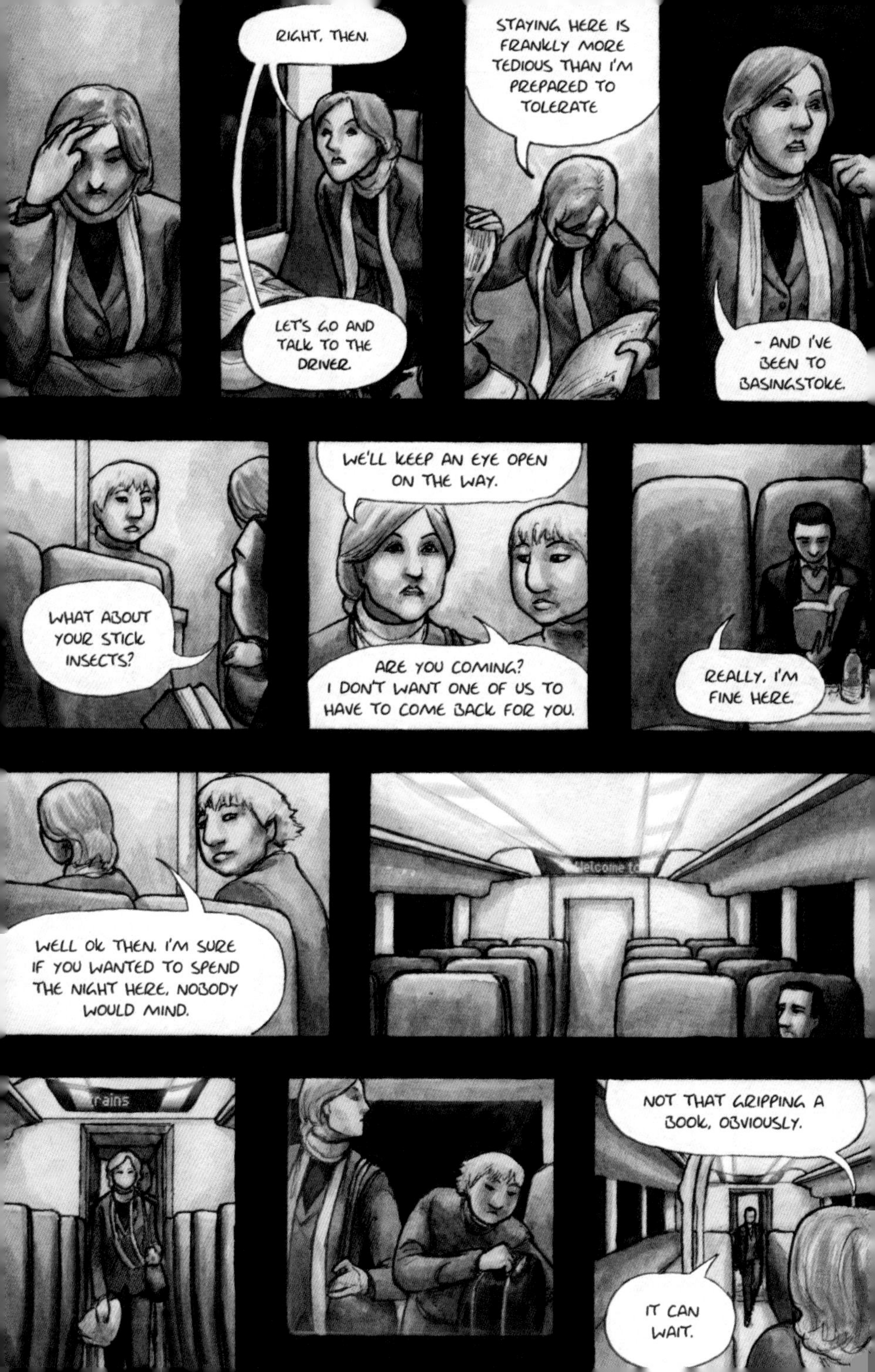
RIGHT, THEN.
LET'S GO AND TALK TO THE DRIVER.
STAYING HERE IS FRANKLY MORE TEDIOUS THAN I'M PREPARED TO TOLERATE
- AND I'VE BEEN TO BASINGSTOKE.
WHAT ABOUT YOUR STICK INSECTS?
WE'LL KEEP AN EYE OPEN ON THE WAY.
ARE YOU COMING? I DON'T WANT ONE OF US TO HAVE TO COME BACK FOR YOU.
REALLY, I'M FINE HERE.
WELL OK THEN. I'M SURE IF YOU WANTED TO SPEND THE NIGHT HERE, NOBODY WOULD MIND.
Welcome to
trains
NOT THAT GRIPPING A BOOK, OBVIOUSLY.
IT CAN WAIT.

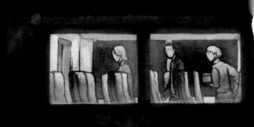

BEEN TRAVELLING SINCE LONDON?

WE'RE NOT TOGETHER.

YES...

I DON'T SUPPOSE YOU TRIED IN HERE, DID YOU?

NO...

HELLO? ANYBODY IN THERE? ANY GUARDS? ANY INSECTS?

WON'T BE A MINUTE.

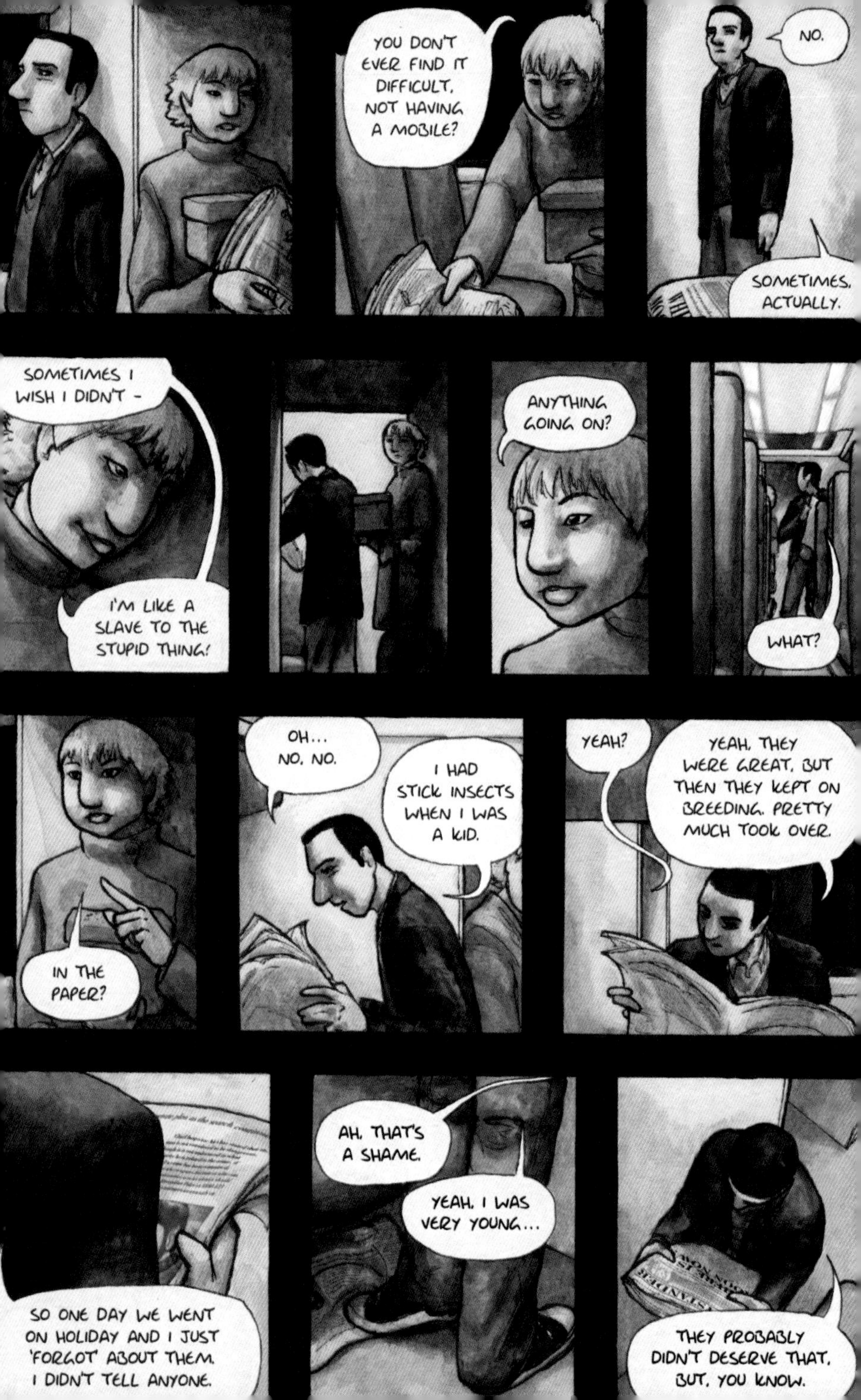
YOU DON'T EVER FIND IT DIFFICULT, NOT HAVING A MOBILE?
NO.
SOMETIMES, ACTUALLY.
SOMETIMES I WISH I DIDN'T -
I'M LIKE A SLAVE TO THE STUPID THING!
ANYTHING GOING ON?
WHAT?
IN THE PAPER?
OH... NO, NO.
I HAD STICK INSECTS WHEN I WAS A KID.
YEAH?
YEAH, THEY WERE GREAT, BUT THEN THEY KEPT ON BREEDING. PRETTY MUCH TOOK OVER.
SO ONE DAY WE WENT ON HOLIDAY AND I JUST 'FORGOT' ABOUT THEM. I DIDN'T TELL ANYONE.
AH, THAT'S A SHAME.
YEAH, I WAS VERY YOUNG...
THEY PROBABLY DIDN'T DESERVE THAT, BUT, YOU KNOW.

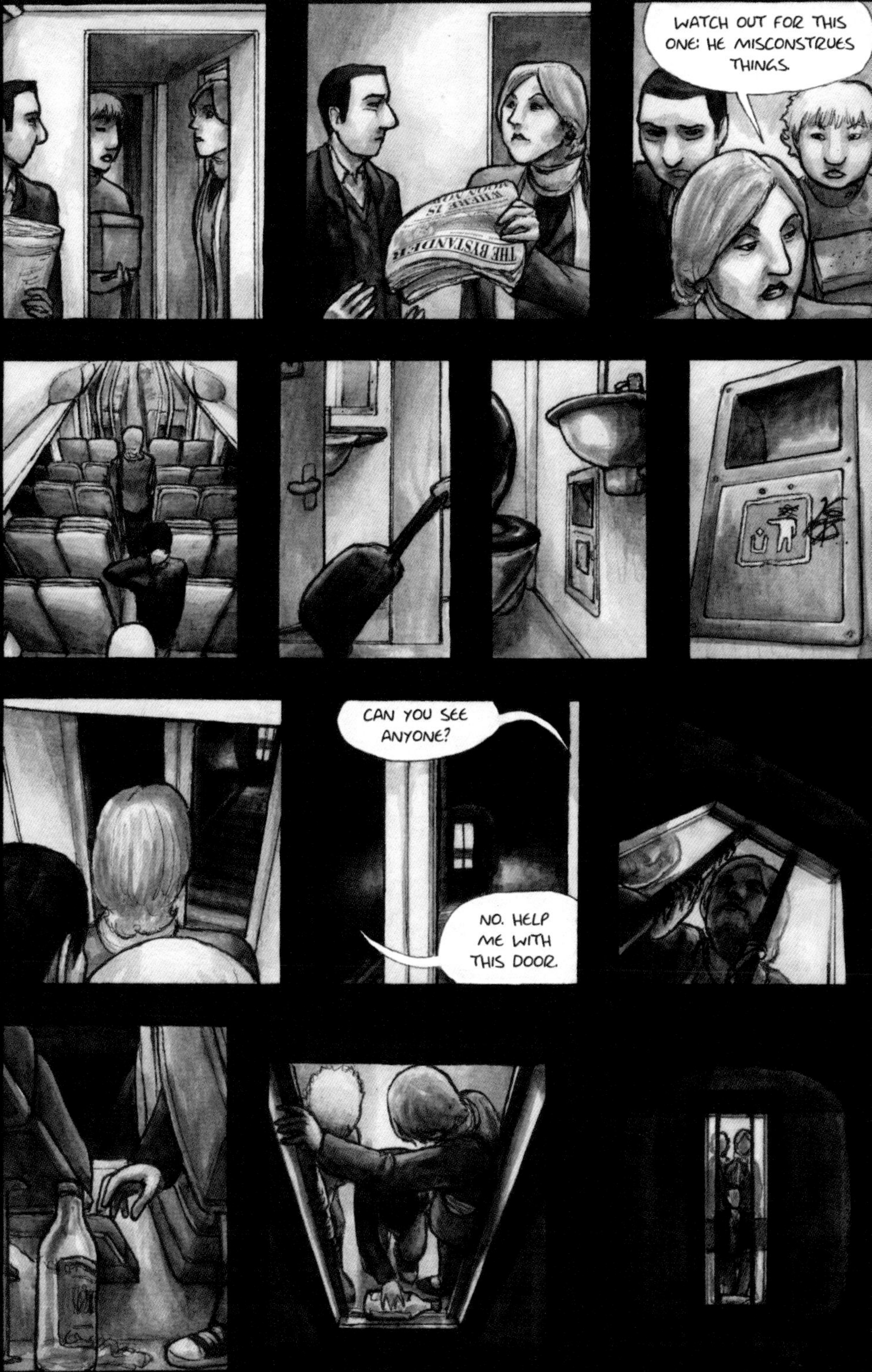
THE BYSTANDER
WHERE IS
WATCH OUT FOR THIS ONE: HE MISCONSTRUES THINGS.
CAN YOU SEE ANYONE?
NO. HELP ME WITH THIS DOOR.

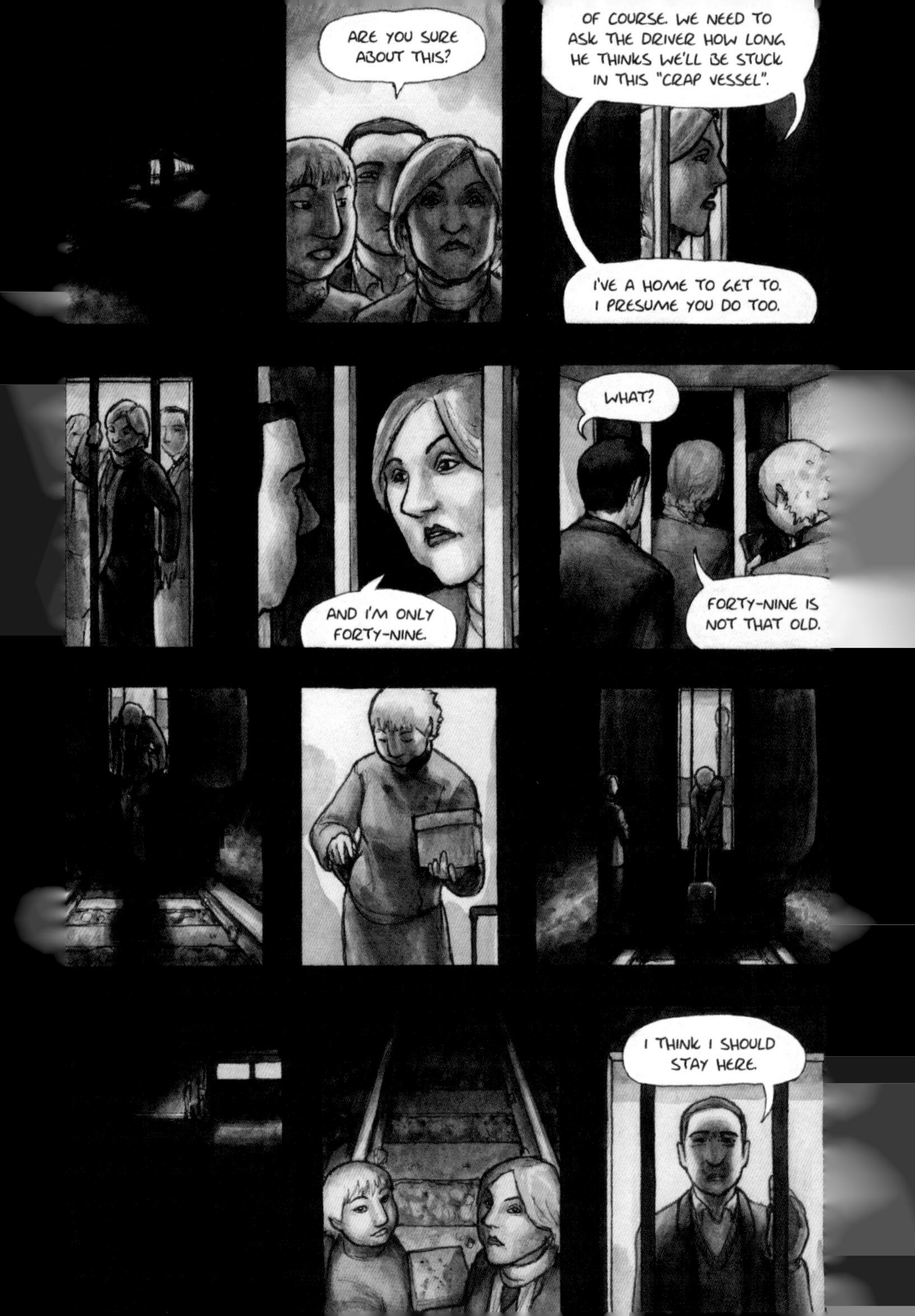

ARE YOU SURE ABOUT THIS?
OF COURSE. WE NEED TO ASK THE DRIVER HOW LONG HE THINKS WE'LL BE STUCK IN THIS "CRAP VESSEL".
I'VE A HOME TO GET TO. I PRESUME YOU DO TOO.
AND I'M ONLY FORTY-NINE.
WHAT?
FORTY-NINE IS NOT THAT OLD.
I THINK I SHOULD STAY HERE.

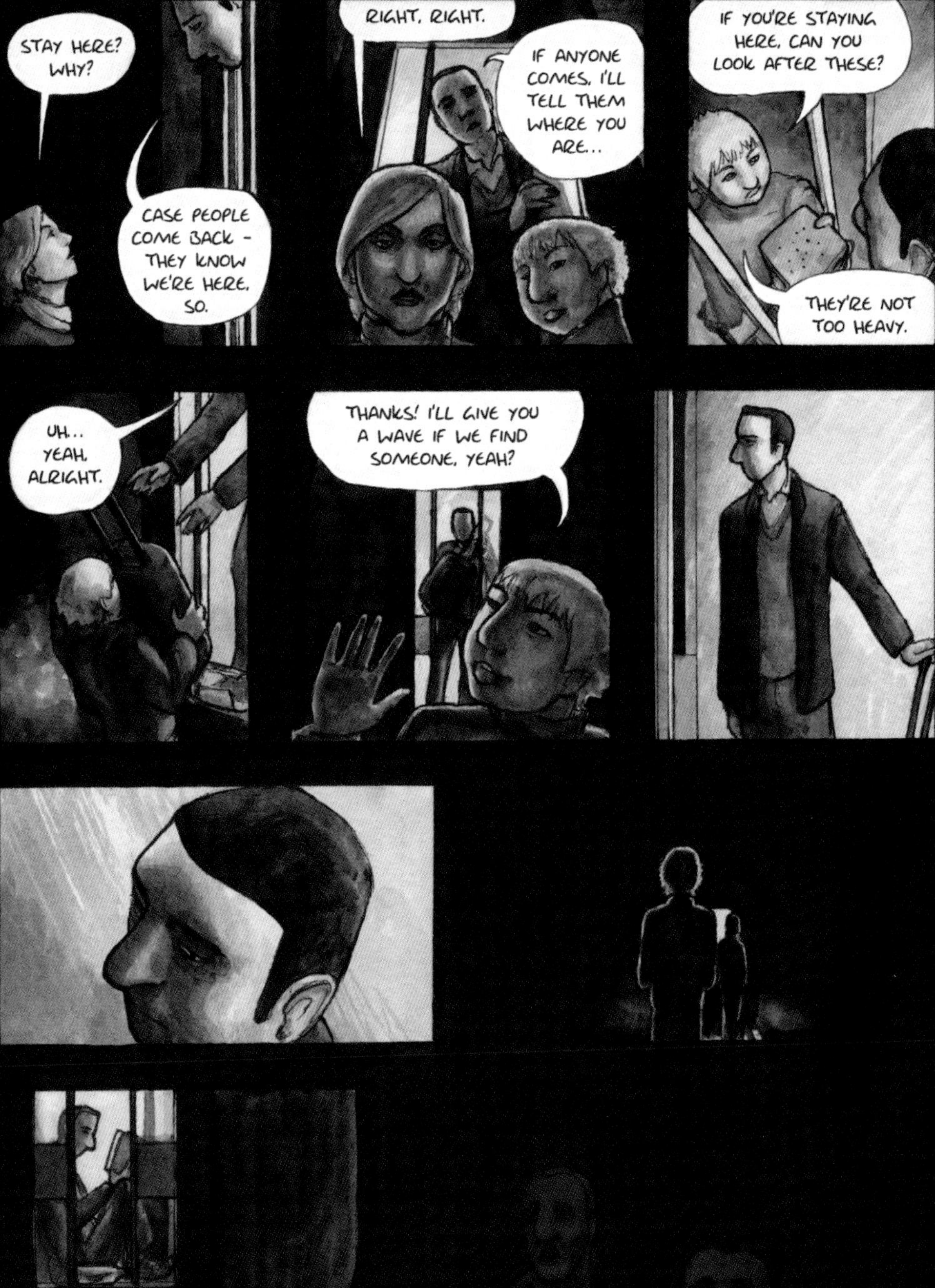
STAY HERE? WHY?
CASE PEOPLE COME BACK - THEY KNOW WE'RE HERE. SO.
RIGHT, RIGHT.
IF ANYONE COMES, I'LL TELL THEM WHERE YOU ARE...
IF YOU'RE STAYING HERE, CAN YOU LOOK AFTER THESE?
THEY'RE NOT TOO HEAVY.
UH... YEAH, ALRIGHT.
THANKS! I'LL GIVE YOU A WAVE IF WE FIND SOMEONE, YEAH?

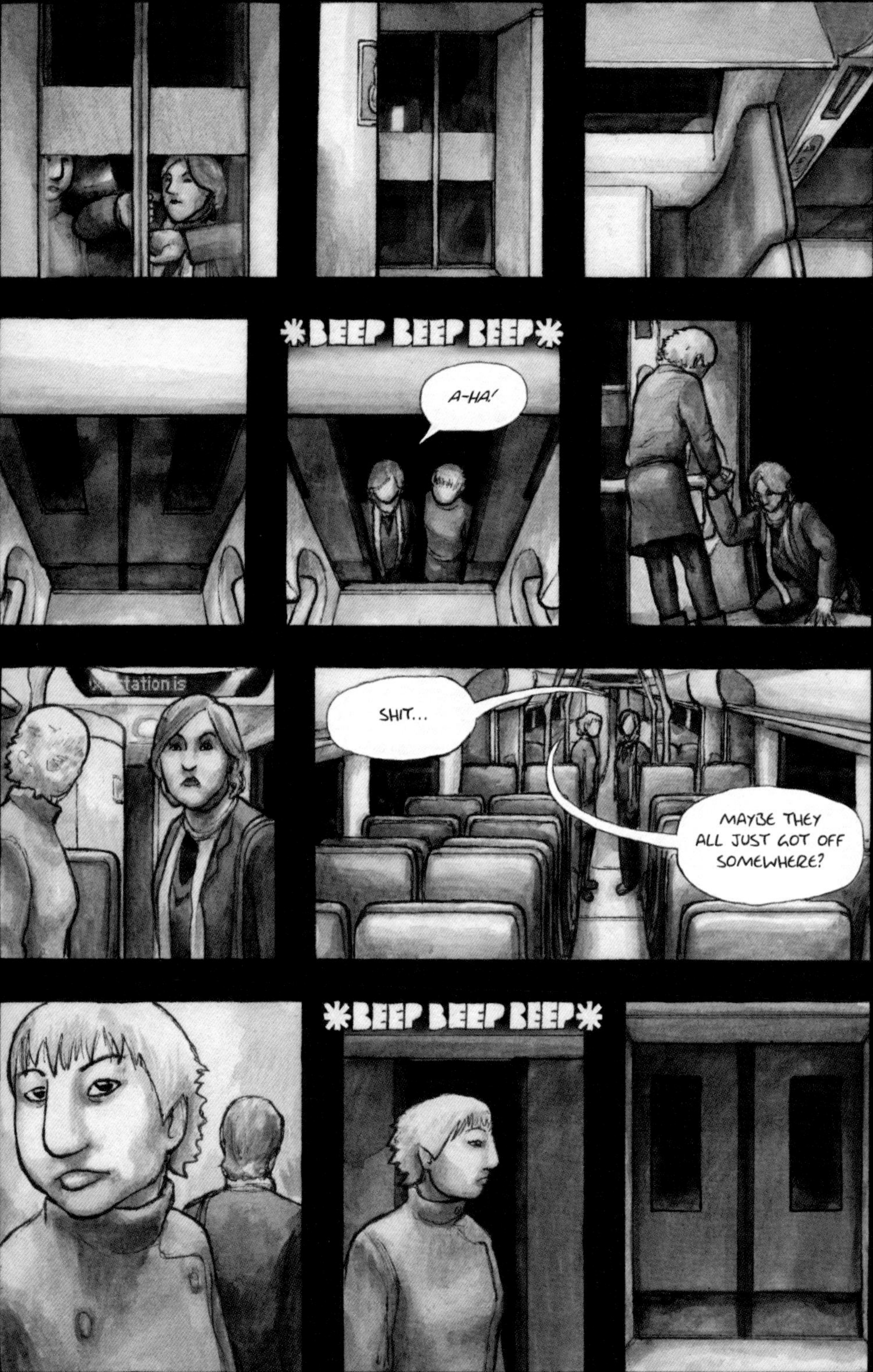
BEEP BEEP BEEP
A-HA!
station is
SHIT...
MAYBE THEY ALL JUST GOT OFF SOMEWHERE?
BEEP BEEP BEEP

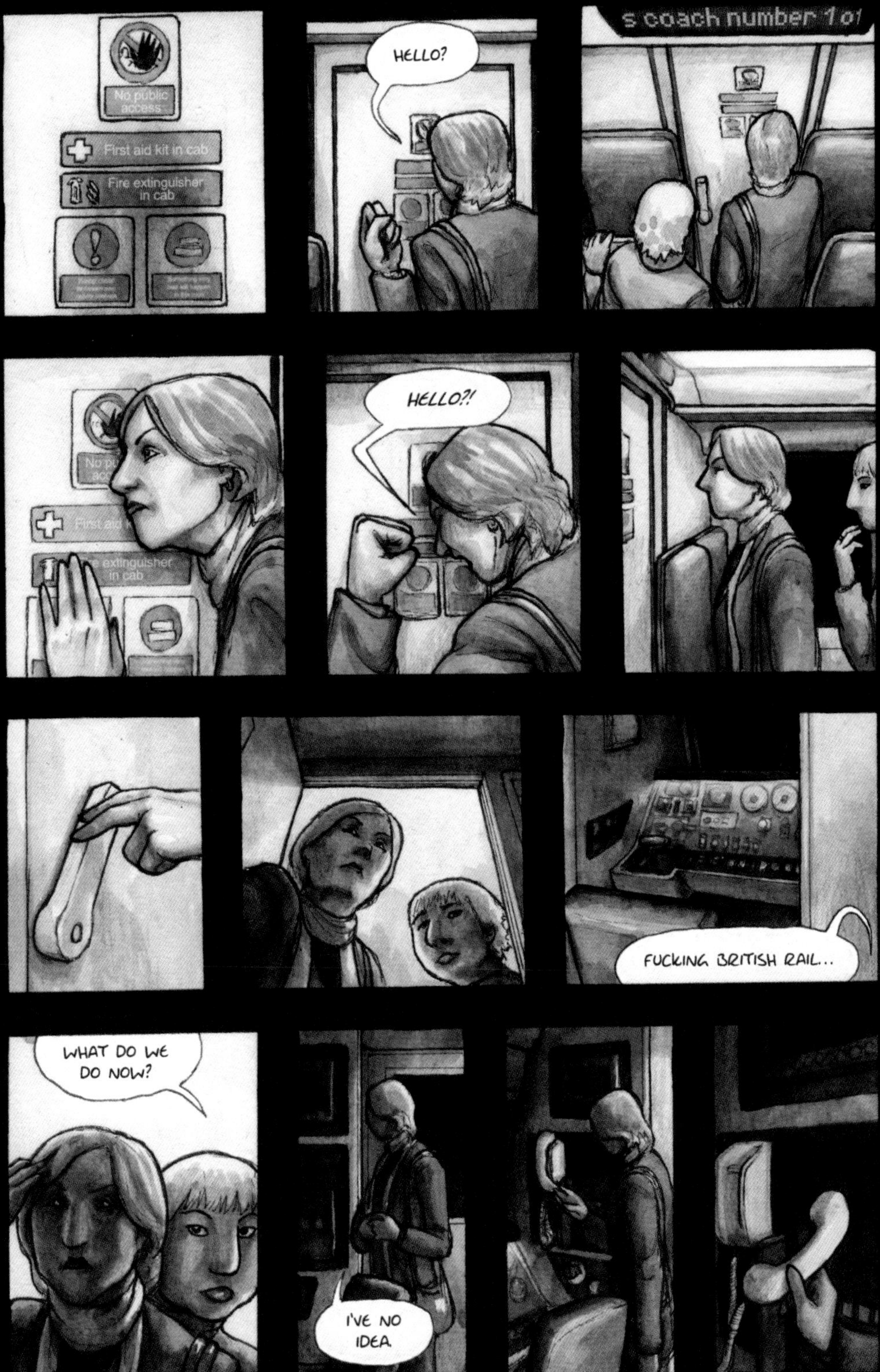
No public access
First aid kit in cab
Fire extinguisher in cab
HELLO?
s coach number 1 of
HELLO?!
FUCKING BRITISH RAIL...
WHAT DO WE DO NOW?
I'VE NO IDEA

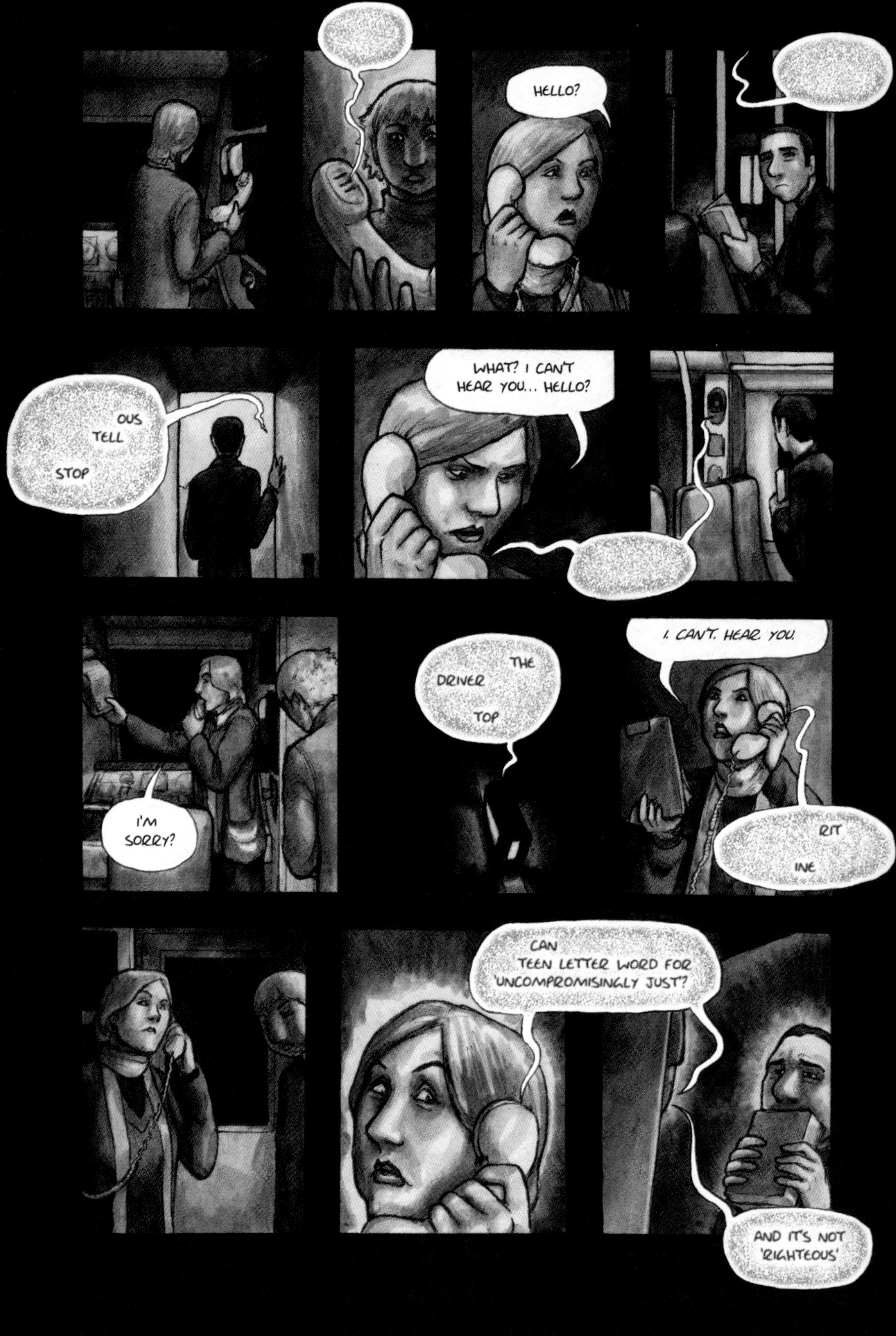
HELLO?
OUS
TELL
STOP
WHAT? I CAN'T HEAR YOU... HELLO?
I'M SORRY?
THE
DRIVER
TOP
I. CAN'T. HEAR. YOU.
RIT
INE
CAN
TEEN LETTER WORD FOR 'UNCOMPROMISINGLY JUST'?
AND IT'S NOT 'RIGHTEOUS'

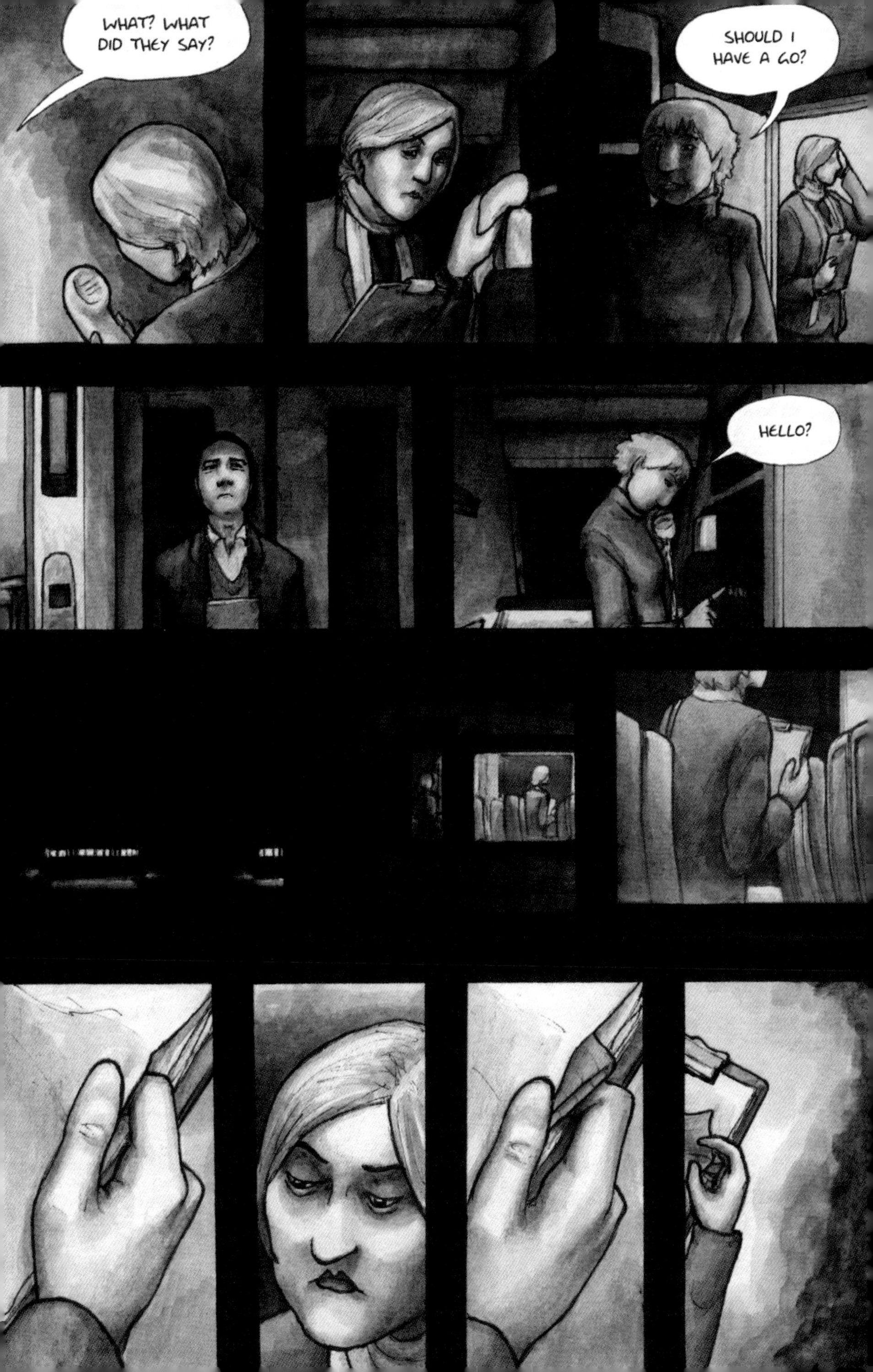
WHAT? WHAT DID THEY SAY?
SHOULD I HAVE A GO?
HELLO?

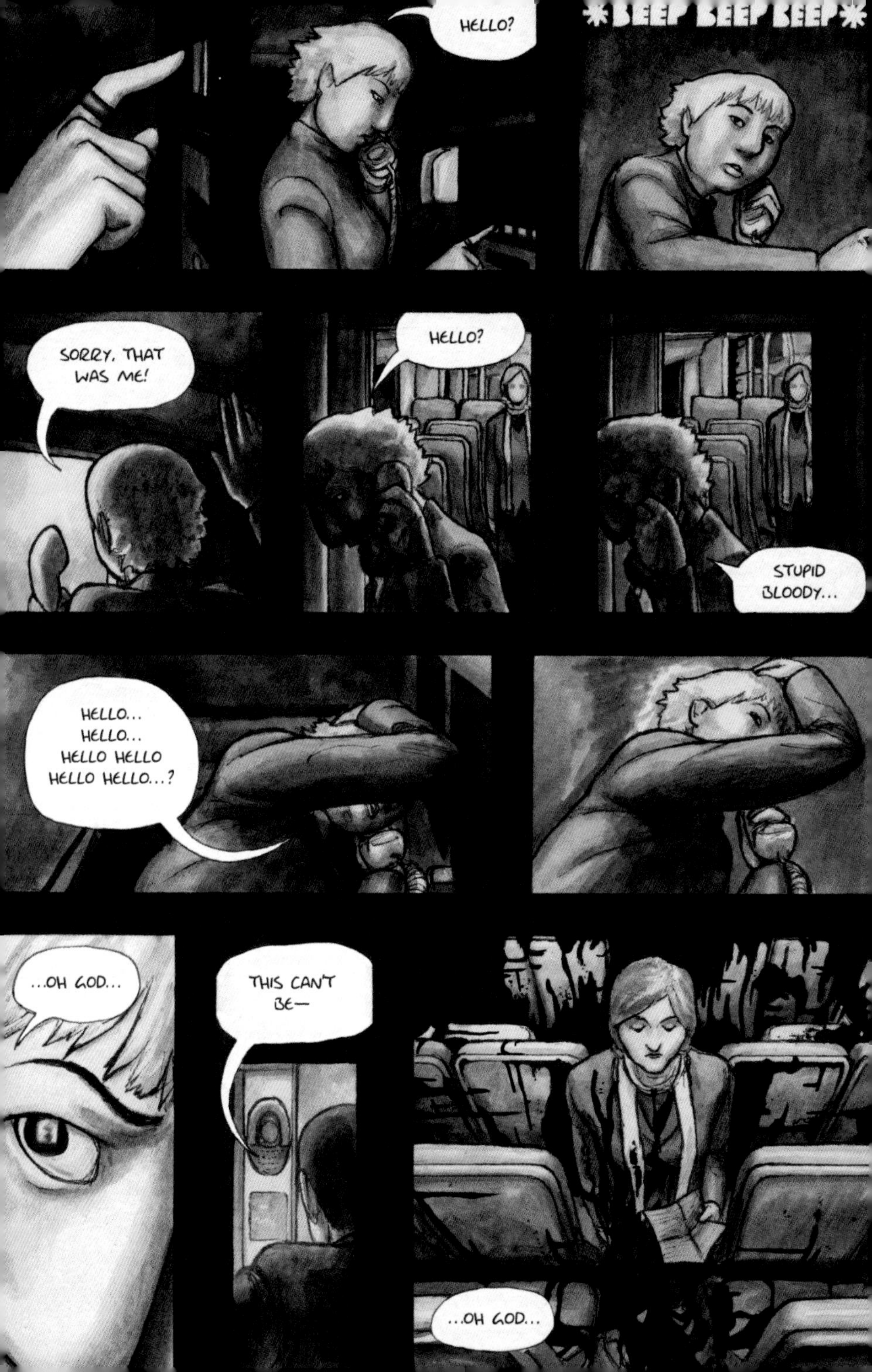
HELLO?
BEEP BEEP BEEP
SORRY, THAT WAS ME!
HELLO?
STUPID BLOODY...
HELLO... HELLO... HELLO HELLO HELLO HELLO...?
...OH GOD...
THIS CAN'T BE—
...OH GOD...

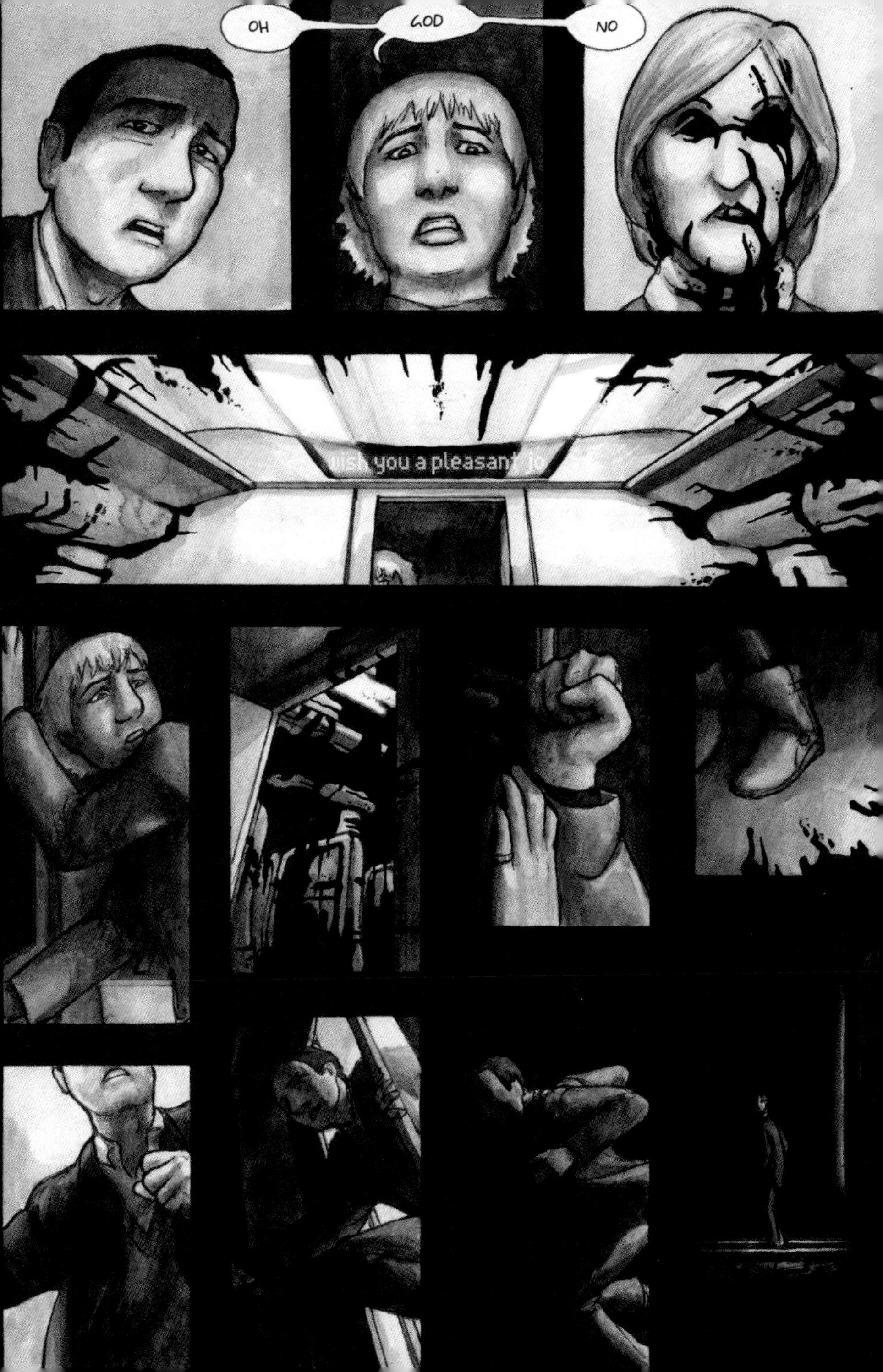
OH
GOD
NO
wish you a pleasant jo

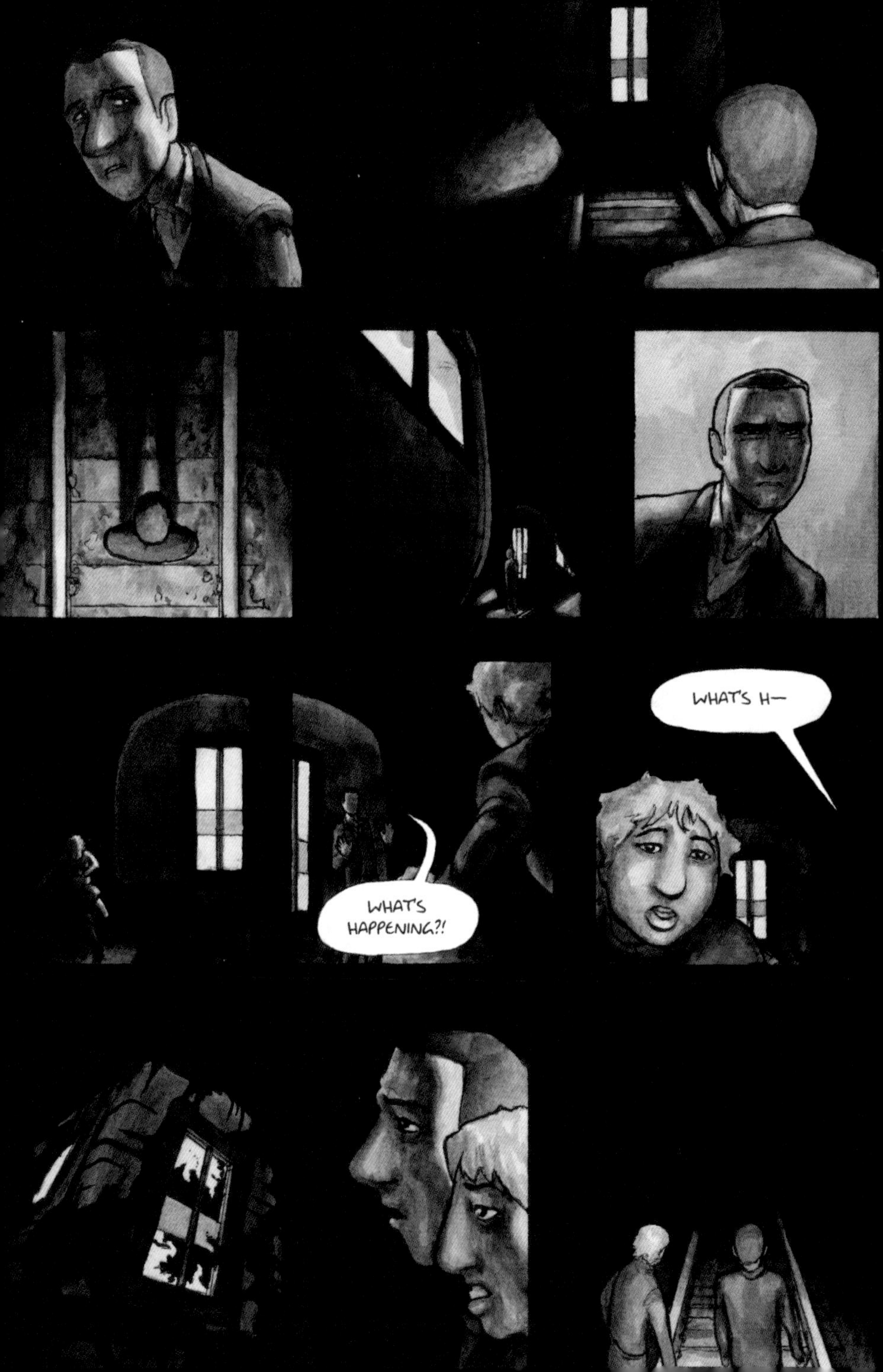
WHAT'S HAPPENING?!
WHAT'S H—

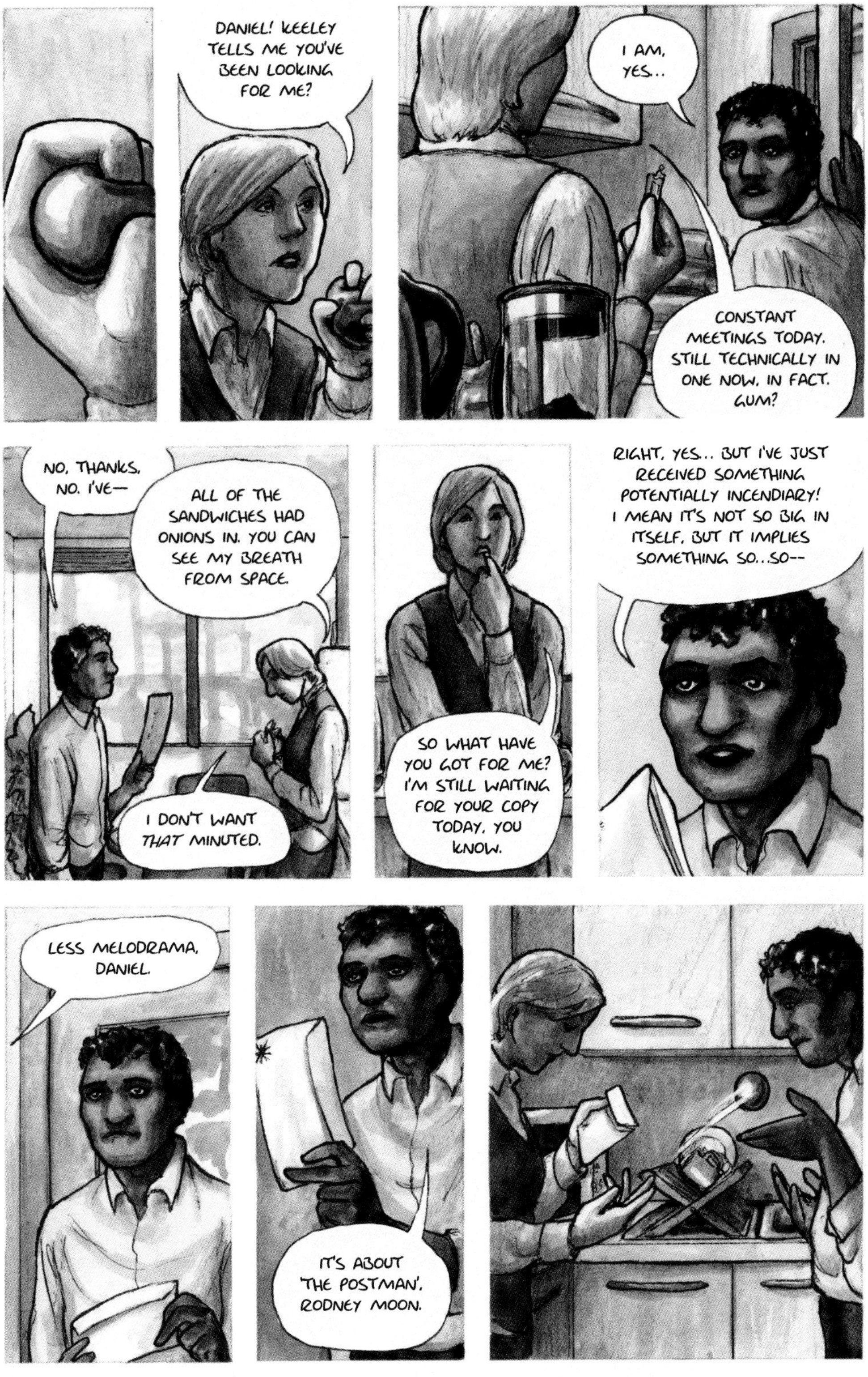
DANIEL! KEELEY TELLS ME YOU'VE BEEN LOOKING FOR ME?
I AM, YES...
CONSTANT MEETINGS TODAY. STILL TECHNICALLY IN ONE NOW, IN FACT. GUM?
NO, THANKS. NO. I'VE—
ALL OF THE SANDWICHES HAD ONIONS IN. YOU CAN SEE MY BREATH FROM SPACE.
I DON'T WANT *THAT* MINUTED.
SO WHAT HAVE YOU GOT FOR ME? I'M STILL WAITING FOR YOUR COPY TODAY, YOU KNOW.
RIGHT, YES... BUT I'VE JUST RECEIVED SOMETHING POTENTIALLY INCENDIARY! I MEAN IT'S NOT SO BIG IN ITSELF, BUT IT IMPLIES SOMETHING SO...SO--
LESS MELODRAMA, DANIEL.
IT'S ABOUT 'THE POSTMAN', RODNEY MOON.

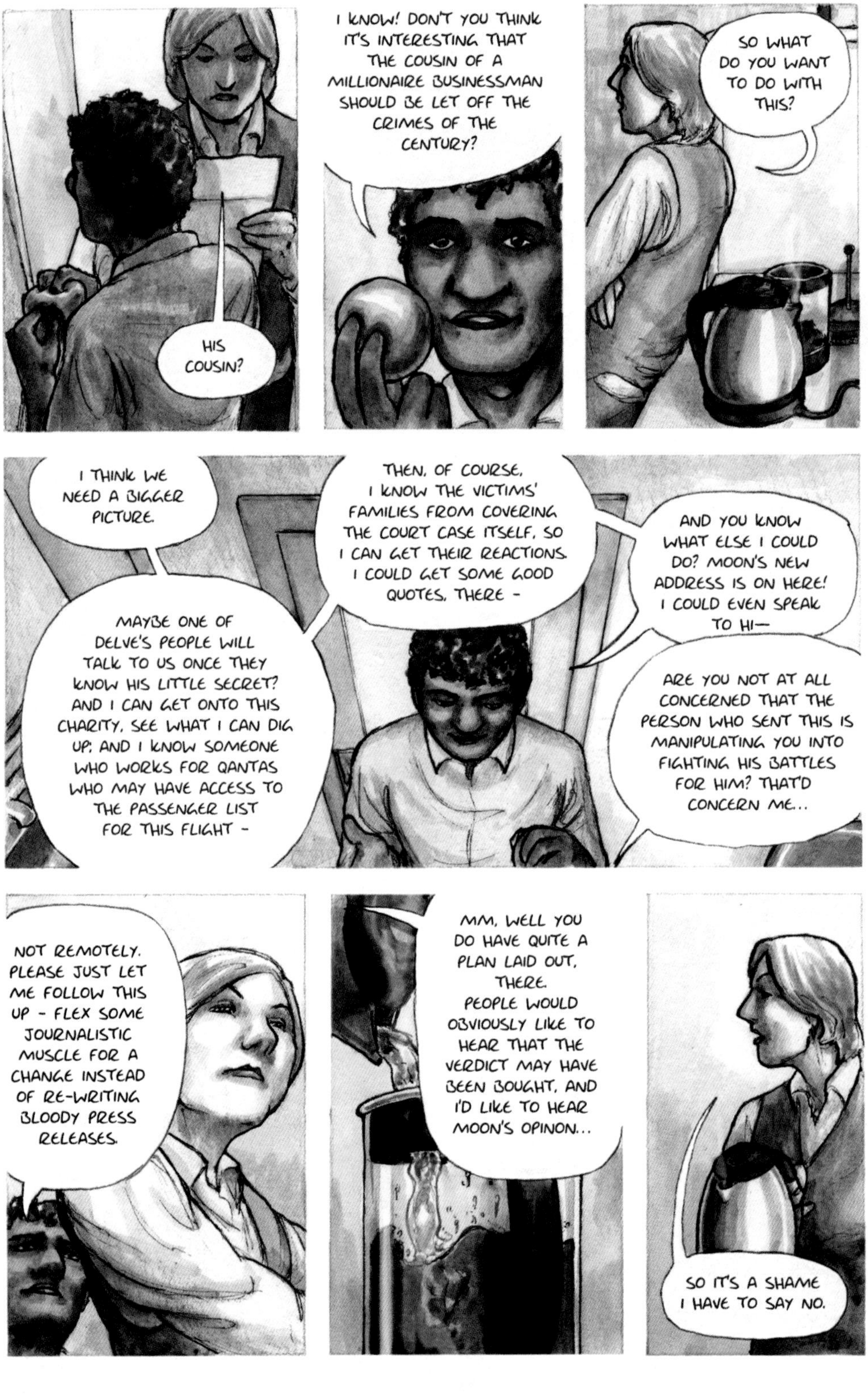
HIS COUSIN?
I KNOW! DON'T YOU THINK IT'S INTERESTING THAT THE COUSIN OF A MILLIONAIRE BUSINESSMAN SHOULD BE LET OFF THE CRIMES OF THE CENTURY?
SO WHAT DO YOU WANT TO DO WITH THIS?
I THINK WE NEED A BIGGER PICTURE.
MAYBE ONE OF DELVE'S PEOPLE WILL TALK TO US ONCE THEY KNOW HIS LITTLE SECRET? AND I CAN GET ONTO THIS CHARITY, SEE WHAT I CAN DIG UP; AND I KNOW SOMEONE WHO WORKS FOR QANTAS WHO MAY HAVE ACCESS TO THE PASSENGER LIST FOR THIS FLIGHT -
THEN, OF COURSE, I KNOW THE VICTIMS' FAMILIES FROM COVERING THE COURT CASE ITSELF, SO I CAN GET THEIR REACTIONS. I COULD GET SOME GOOD QUOTES, THERE -
AND YOU KNOW WHAT ELSE I COULD DO? MOON'S NEW ADDRESS IS ON HERE! I COULD EVEN SPEAK TO HI—
ARE YOU NOT AT ALL CONCERNED THAT THE PERSON WHO SENT THIS IS MANIPULATING YOU INTO FIGHTING HIS BATTLES FOR HIM? THAT'D CONCERN ME...
NOT REMOTELY. PLEASE JUST LET ME FOLLOW THIS UP - FLEX SOME JOURNALISTIC MUSCLE FOR A CHANGE INSTEAD OF RE-WRITING BLOODY PRESS RELEASES.
MM, WELL YOU DO HAVE QUITE A PLAN LAID OUT, THERE. PEOPLE WOULD OBVIOUSLY LIKE TO HEAR THAT THE VERDICT MAY HAVE BEEN BOUGHT, AND I'D LIKE TO HEAR MOON'S OPINON...
SO IT'S A SHAME I HAVE TO SAY NO.

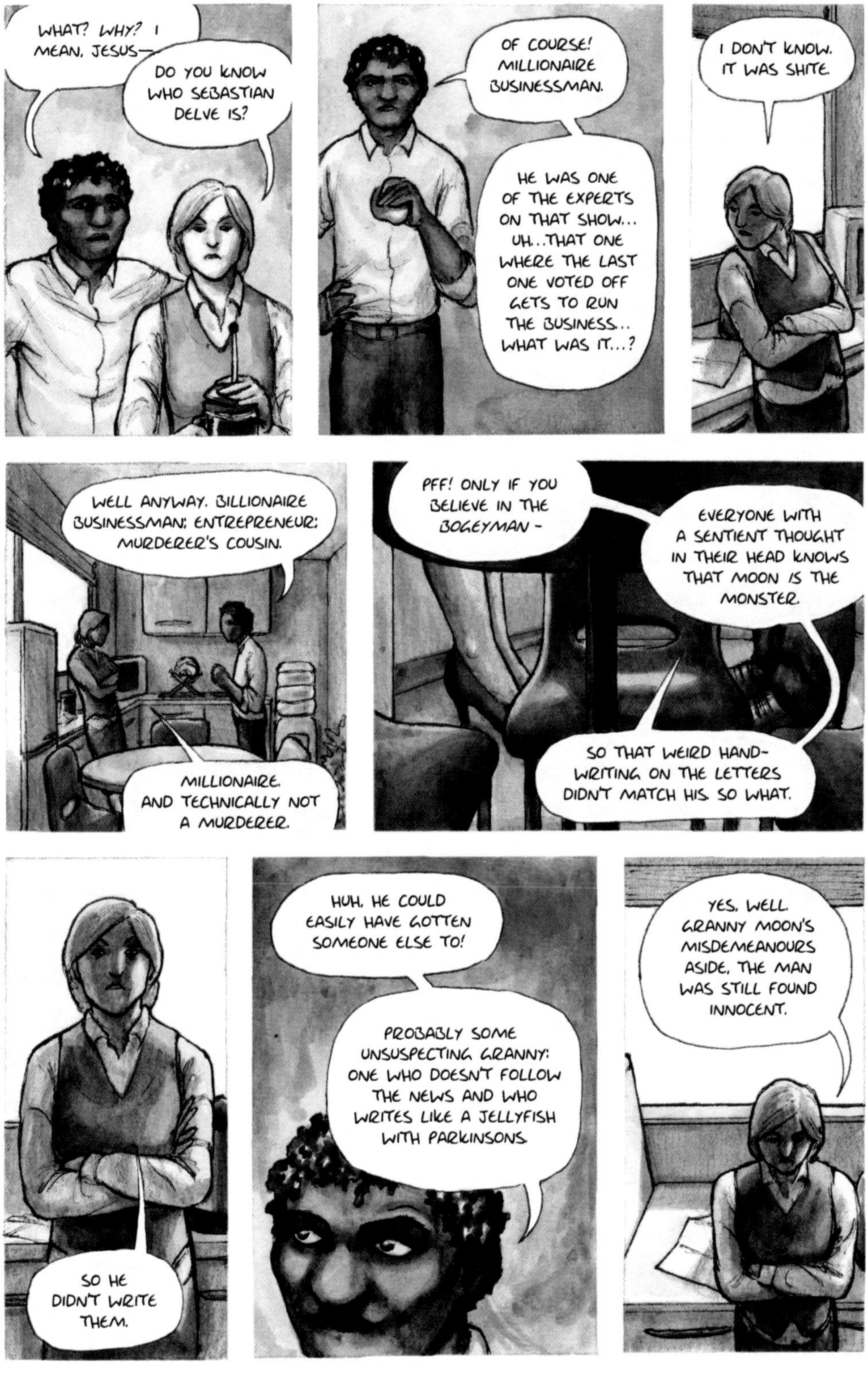
WHAT? WHY? I MEAN, JESUS—
DO YOU KNOW WHO SEBASTIAN DELVE IS?
OF COURSE! MILLIONAIRE BUSINESSMAN.
HE WAS ONE OF THE EXPERTS ON THAT SHOW... UH...THAT ONE WHERE THE LAST ONE VOTED OFF GETS TO RUN THE BUSINESS... WHAT WAS IT...?
I DON'T KNOW. IT WAS SHITE.
WELL ANYWAY. BILLIONAIRE BUSINESSMAN; ENTREPRENEUR; MURDERER'S COUSIN.
MILLIONAIRE. AND TECHNICALLY NOT A MURDERER.
PFF! ONLY IF YOU BELIEVE IN THE BOGEYMAN -
EVERYONE WITH A SENTIENT THOUGHT IN THEIR HEAD KNOWS THAT MOON IS THE MONSTER.
SO THAT WEIRD HAND-WRITING ON THE LETTERS DIDN'T MATCH HIS. SO WHAT.
SO HE DIDN'T WRITE THEM.
HUH, HE COULD EASILY HAVE GOTTEN SOMEONE ELSE TO!
PROBABLY SOME UNSUSPECTING GRANNY: ONE WHO DOESN'T FOLLOW THE NEWS AND WHO WRITES LIKE A JELLYFISH WITH PARKINSONS.
YES, WELL. GRANNY MOON'S MISDEMEANOURS ASIDE, THE MAN WAS STILL FOUND INNOCENT.

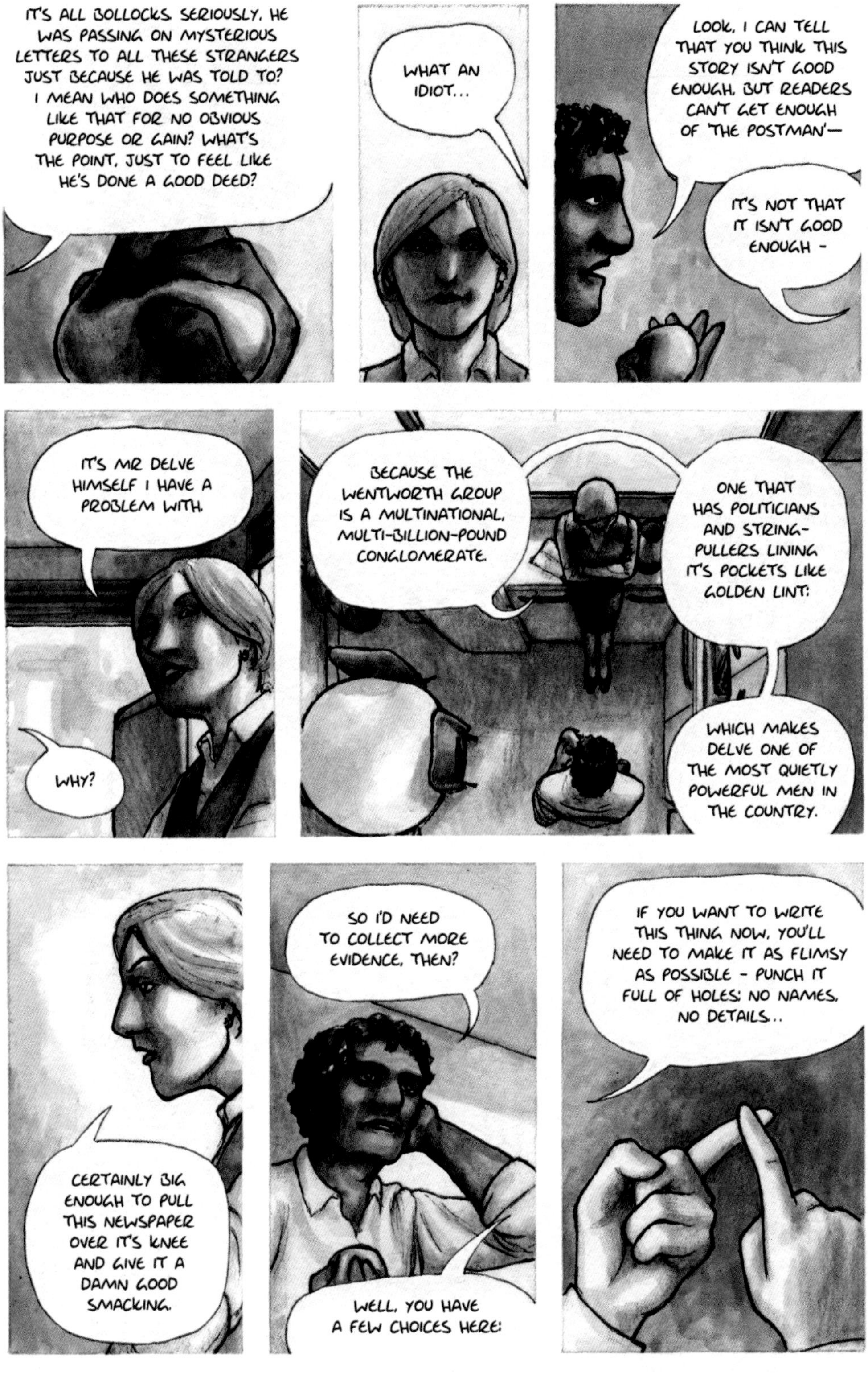
IT'S ALL BOLLOCKS SERIOUSLY. HE WAS PASSING ON MYSTERIOUS LETTERS TO ALL THESE STRANGERS JUST BECAUSE HE WAS TOLD TO? I MEAN WHO DOES SOMETHING LIKE THAT FOR NO OBVIOUS PURPOSE OR GAIN? WHAT'S THE POINT, JUST TO FEEL LIKE HE'S DONE A GOOD DEED?
WHAT AN IDIOT...
LOOK, I CAN TELL THAT YOU THINK THIS STORY ISN'T GOOD ENOUGH, BUT READERS CAN'T GET ENOUGH OF 'THE POSTMAN'—
IT'S NOT THAT IT ISN'T GOOD ENOUGH -
IT'S MR DELVE HIMSELF I HAVE A PROBLEM WITH.
WHY?
BECAUSE THE WENTWORTH GROUP IS A MULTINATIONAL, MULTI-BILLION-POUND CONGLOMERATE.
ONE THAT HAS POLITICIANS AND STRING-PULLERS LINING IT'S POCKETS LIKE GOLDEN LINT:
WHICH MAKES DELVE ONE OF THE MOST QUIETLY POWERFUL MEN IN THE COUNTRY.
CERTAINLY BIG ENOUGH TO PULL THIS NEWSPAPER OVER IT'S KNEE AND GIVE IT A DAMN GOOD SMACKING.
SO I'D NEED TO COLLECT MORE EVIDENCE, THEN?
WELL, YOU HAVE A FEW CHOICES HERE:
IF YOU WANT TO WRITE THIS THING NOW, YOU'LL NEED TO MAKE IT AS FLIMSY AS POSSIBLE - PUNCH IT FULL OF HOLES: NO NAMES, NO DETAILS...

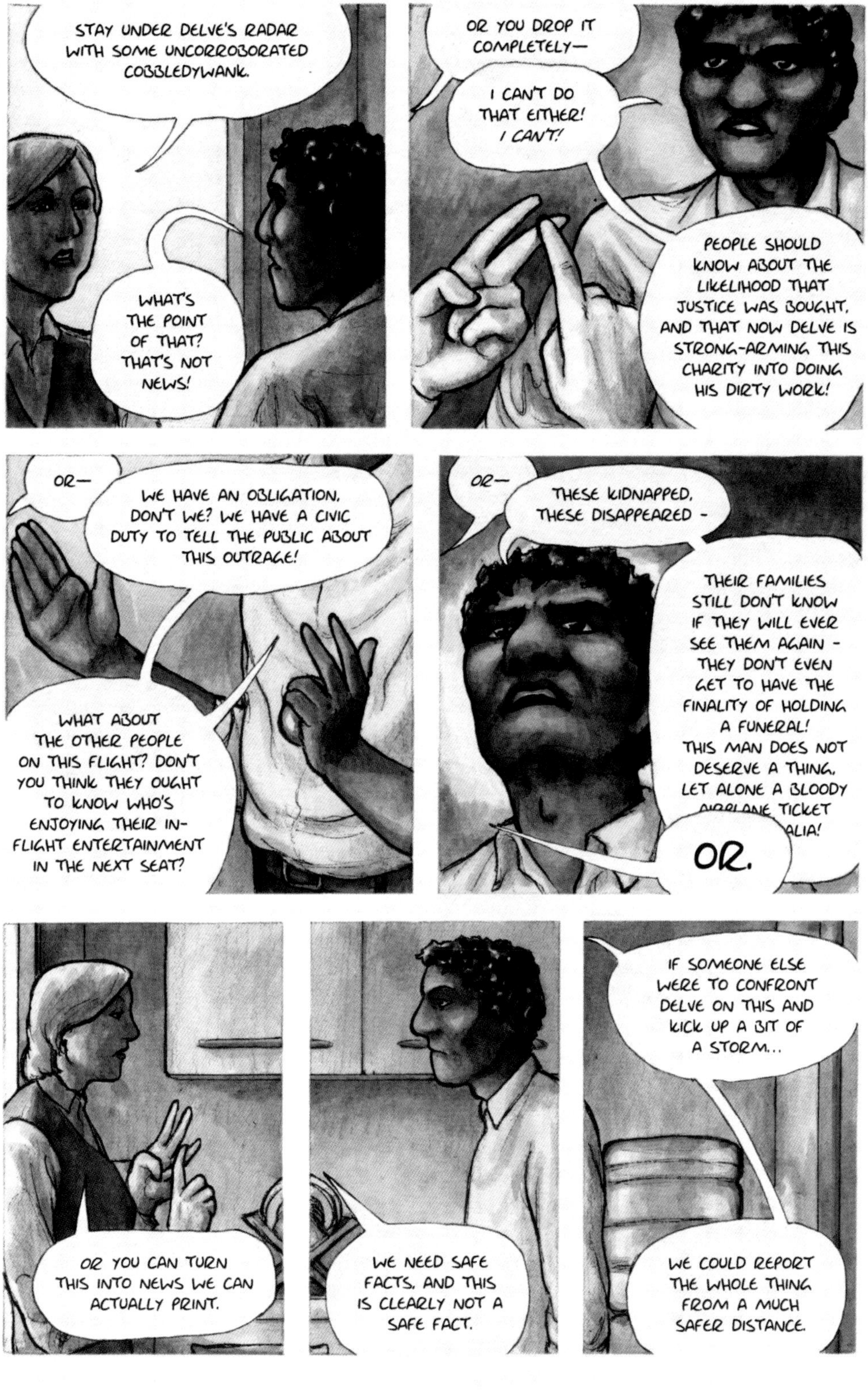
STAY UNDER DELVE'S RADAR WITH SOME UNCORROBORATED COBBLEDYWANK.
WHAT'S THE POINT OF THAT? THAT'S NOT NEWS!
OR YOU DROP IT COMPLETELY—
I CAN'T DO THAT EITHER! I CAN'T!
PEOPLE SHOULD KNOW ABOUT THE LIKELIHOOD THAT JUSTICE WAS BOUGHT, AND THAT NOW DELVE IS STRONG-ARMING THIS CHARITY INTO DOING HIS DIRTY WORK!
OR—
WE HAVE AN OBLIGATION, DON'T WE? WE HAVE A CIVIC DUTY TO TELL THE PUBLIC ABOUT THIS OUTRAGE!
WHAT ABOUT THE OTHER PEOPLE ON THIS FLIGHT? DON'T YOU THINK THEY OUGHT TO KNOW WHO'S ENJOYING THEIR IN-FLIGHT ENTERTAINMENT IN THE NEXT SEAT?
OR—
THESE KIDNAPPED, THESE DISAPPEARED -
THEIR FAMILIES STILL DON'T KNOW IF THEY WILL EVER SEE THEM AGAIN - THEY DON'T EVEN GET TO HAVE THE FINALITY OF HOLDING A FUNERAL! THIS MAN DOES NOT DESERVE A THING, LET ALONE A BLOODY
OR.
OR YOU CAN TURN THIS INTO NEWS WE CAN ACTUALLY PRINT.
WE NEED SAFE FACTS, AND THIS IS CLEARLY NOT A SAFE FACT.
IF SOMEONE ELSE WERE TO CONFRONT DELVE ON THIS AND KICK UP A BIT OF A STORM...
WE COULD REPORT THE WHOLE THING FROM A MUCH SAFER DISTANCE.

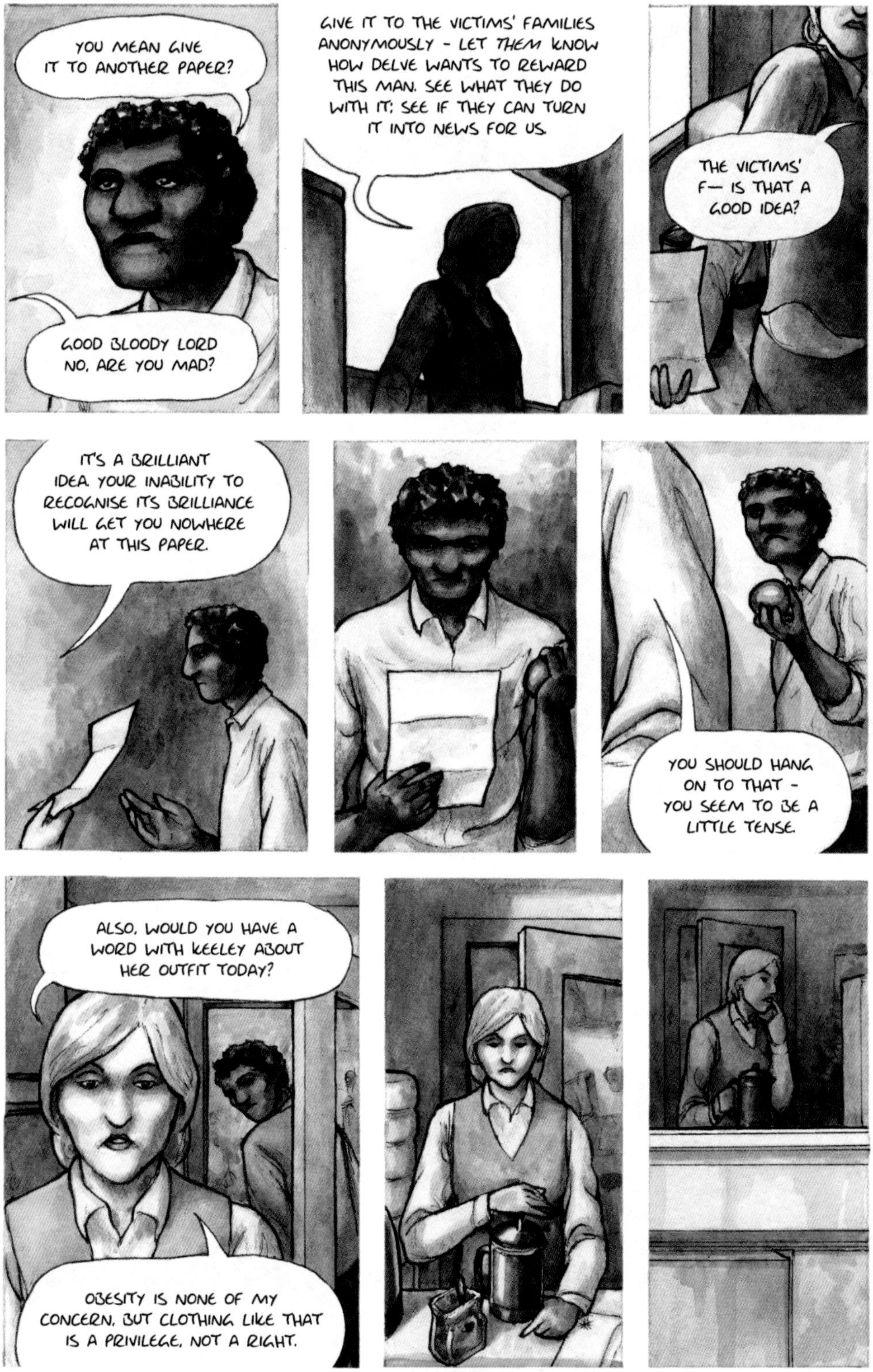
YOU MEAN GIVE IT TO ANOTHER PAPER?
GOOD BLOODY LORD NO, ARE YOU MAD?
GIVE IT TO THE VICTIMS' FAMILIES ANONYMOUSLY - LET THEM KNOW HOW DELVE WANTS TO REWARD THIS MAN. SEE WHAT THEY DO WITH IT; SEE IF THEY CAN TURN IT INTO NEWS FOR US.
THE VICTIMS' F— IS THAT A GOOD IDEA?
IT'S A BRILLIANT IDEA. YOUR INABILITY TO RECOGNISE ITS BRILLIANCE WILL GET YOU NOWHERE AT THIS PAPER.
YOU SHOULD HANG ON TO THAT - YOU SEEM TO BE A LITTLE TENSE.
ALSO, WOULD YOU HAVE A WORD WITH KEELEY ABOUT HER OUTFIT TODAY?
OBESITY IS NONE OF MY CONCERN, BUT CLOTHING LIKE THAT IS A PRIVILEGE, NOT A RIGHT.

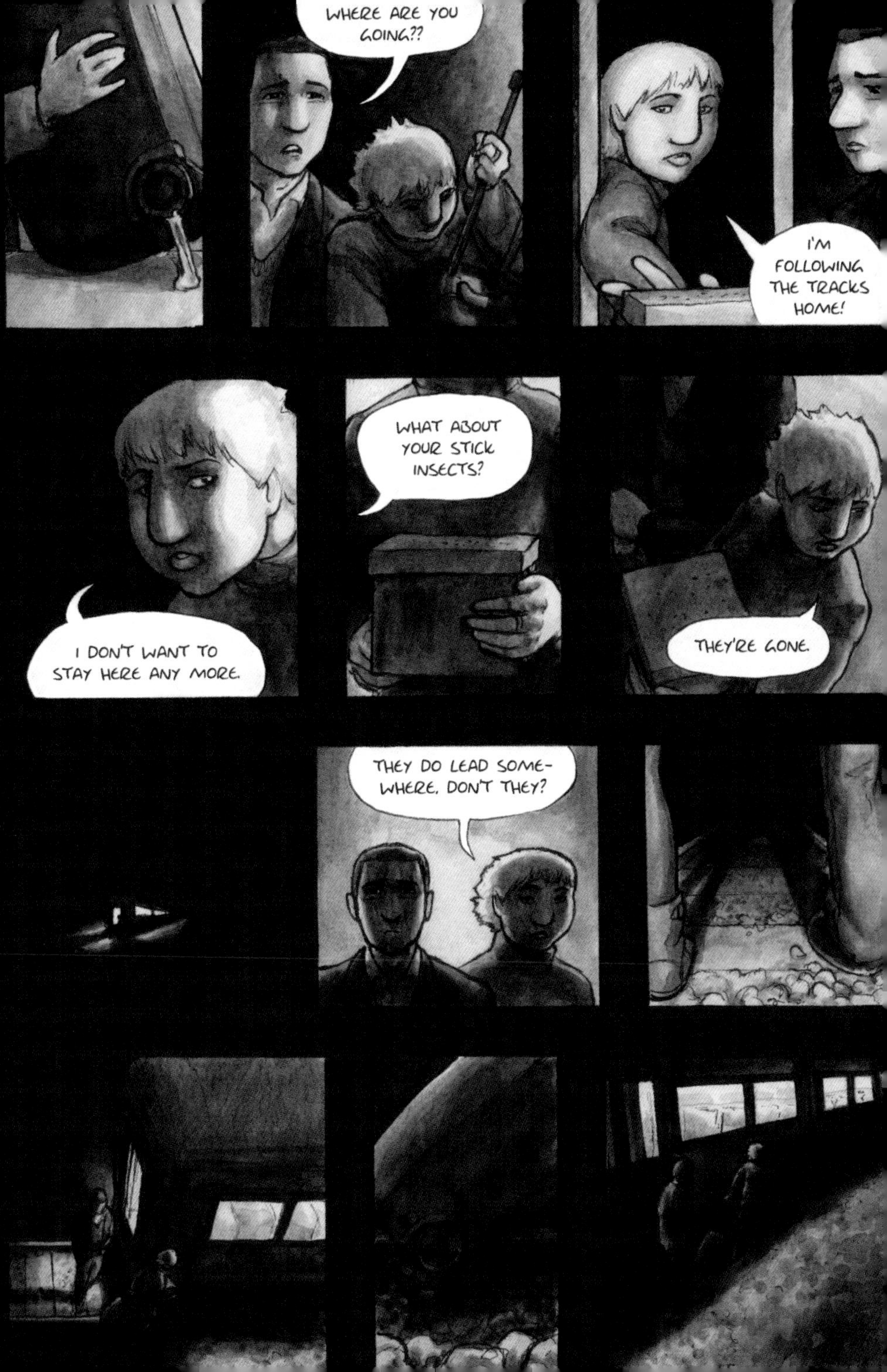
WHERE ARE YOU GOING??
I'M FOLLOWING THE TRACKS HOME!
I DON'T WANT TO STAY HERE ANY MORE.
WHAT ABOUT YOUR STICK INSECTS?
THEY'RE GONE.
THEY DO LEAD SOME-WHERE, DON'T THEY?

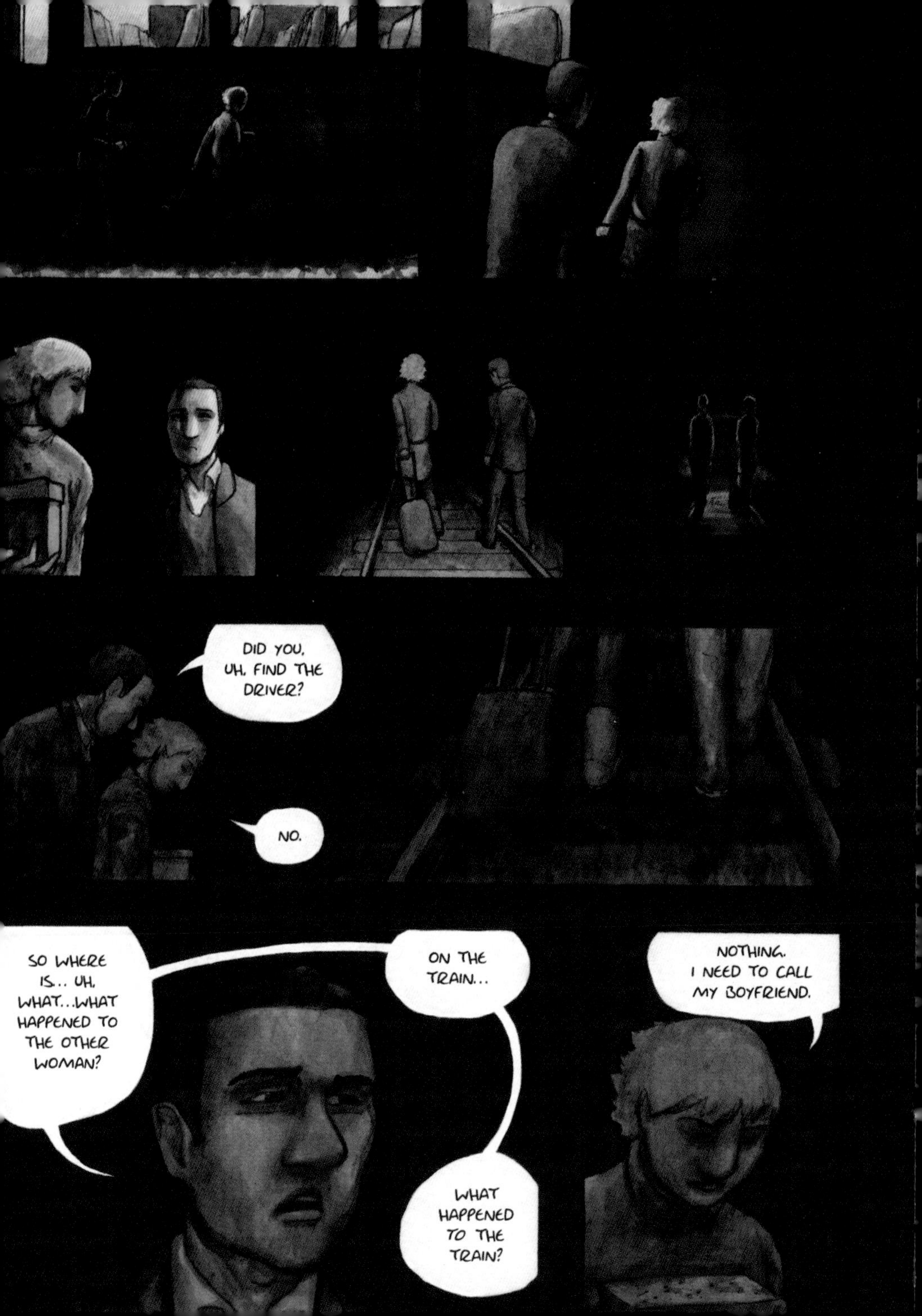
DID YOU, UH, FIND THE DRIVER?
NO.
SO WHERE IS... UH, WHAT...WHAT HAPPENED TO THE OTHER WOMAN?
ON THE TRAIN...
WHAT HAPPENED TO THE TRAIN?
NOTHING. I NEED TO CALL MY BOYFRIEND.

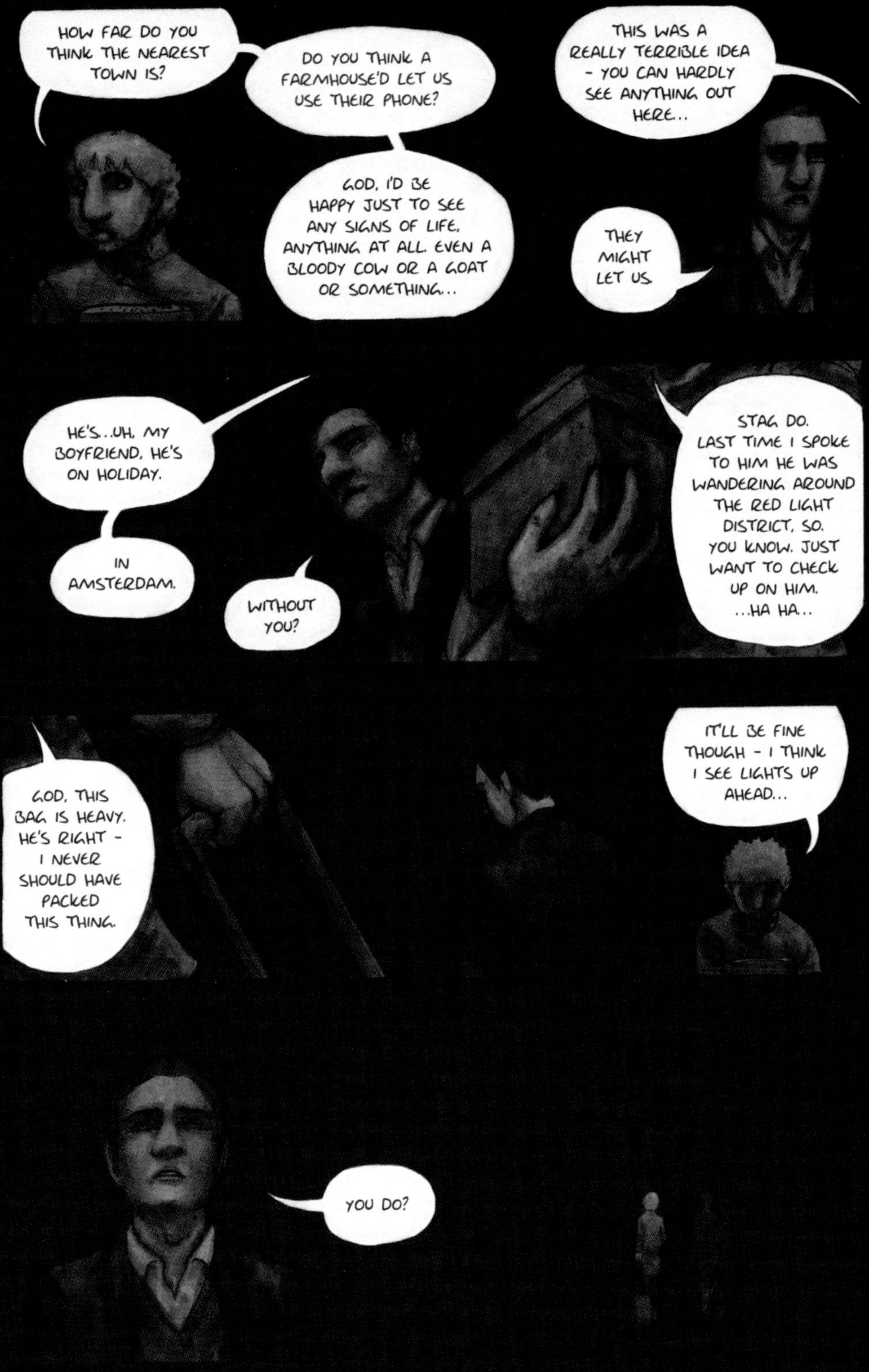
HOW FAR DO YOU THINK THE NEAREST TOWN IS?
DO YOU THINK A FARMHOUSE'D LET US USE THEIR PHONE?
GOD, I'D BE HAPPY JUST TO SEE ANY SIGNS OF LIFE. ANYTHING AT ALL. EVEN A BLOODY COW OR A GOAT OR SOMETHING...
THIS WAS A REALLY TERRIBLE IDEA - YOU CAN HARDLY SEE ANYTHING OUT HERE...
THEY MIGHT LET US.
HE'S...UH, MY BOYFRIEND. HE'S ON HOLIDAY.
IN AMSTERDAM.
WITHOUT YOU?
STAG DO. LAST TIME I SPOKE TO HIM HE WAS WANDERING AROUND THE RED LIGHT DISTRICT, SO. YOU KNOW. JUST WANT TO CHECK UP ON HIM. ...HA HA...
GOD, THIS BAG IS HEAVY. HE'S RIGHT - I NEVER SHOULD HAVE PACKED THIS THING.
IT'LL BE FINE THOUGH - I THINK I SEE LIGHTS UP AHEAD...
YOU DO?

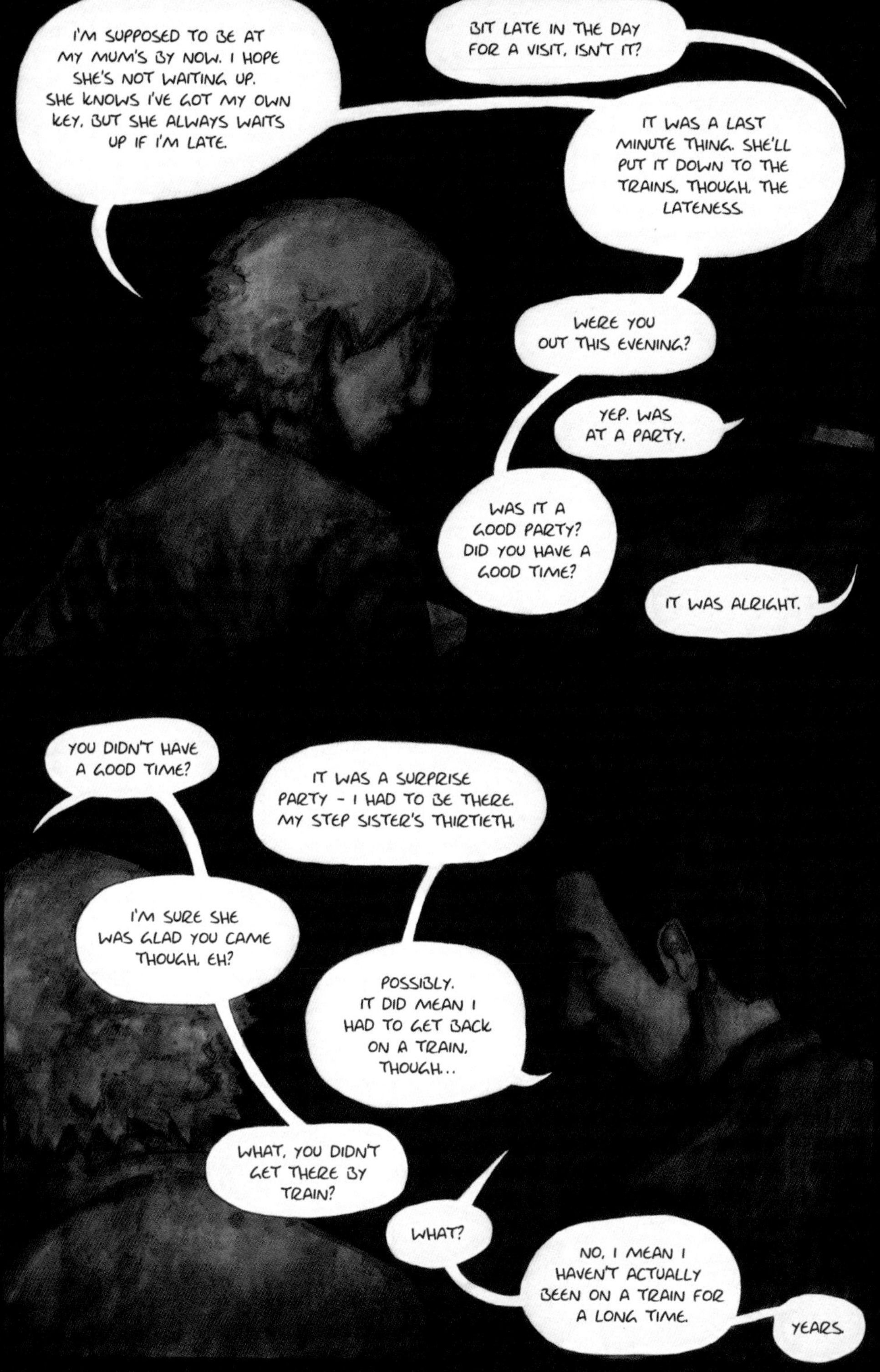
I'M SUPPOSED TO BE AT MY MUM'S BY NOW. I HOPE SHE'S NOT WAITING UP. SHE KNOWS I'VE GOT MY OWN KEY, BUT SHE ALWAYS WAITS UP IF I'M LATE.
BIT LATE IN THE DAY FOR A VISIT, ISN'T IT?
IT WAS A LAST MINUTE THING. SHE'LL PUT IT DOWN TO THE TRAINS, THOUGH, THE LATENESS.
WERE YOU OUT THIS EVENING?
YEP. WAS AT A PARTY.
WAS IT A GOOD PARTY? DID YOU HAVE A GOOD TIME?
IT WAS ALRIGHT.
YOU DIDN'T HAVE A GOOD TIME?
IT WAS A SURPRISE PARTY - I HAD TO BE THERE. MY STEP SISTER'S THIRTIETH.
I'M SURE SHE WAS GLAD YOU CAME THOUGH, EH?
POSSIBLY. IT DID MEAN I HAD TO GET BACK ON A TRAIN, THOUGH...
WHAT, YOU DIDN'T GET THERE BY TRAIN?
WHAT?
NO, I MEAN I HAVEN'T ACTUALLY BEEN ON A TRAIN FOR A LONG TIME.
YEARS.

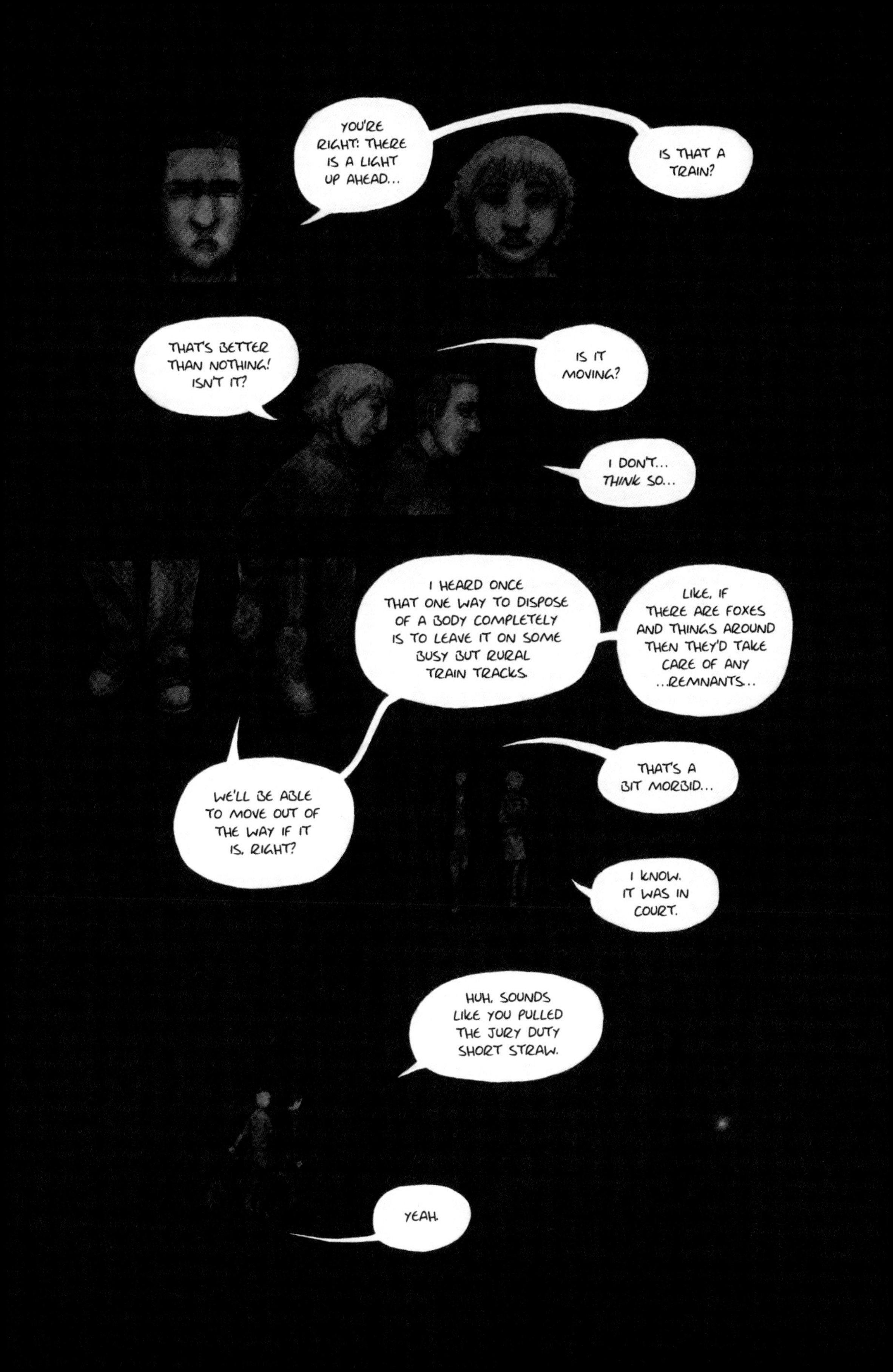
YOU'RE RIGHT: THERE IS A LIGHT UP AHEAD...
IS THAT A TRAIN?
THAT'S BETTER THAN NOTHING! ISN'T IT?
IS IT MOVING?
I DON'T... THINK SO...
I HEARD ONCE THAT ONE WAY TO DISPOSE OF A BODY COMPLETELY IS TO LEAVE IT ON SOME BUSY BUT RURAL TRAIN TRACKS.
LIKE, IF THERE ARE FOXES AND THINGS AROUND THEN THEY'D TAKE CARE OF ANY ...REMNANTS...
WE'LL BE ABLE TO MOVE OUT OF THE WAY IF IT IS, RIGHT?
THAT'S A BIT MORBID...
I KNOW. IT WAS IN COURT.
HUH, SOUNDS LIKE YOU PULLED THE JURY DUTY SHORT STRAW.
YEAH.

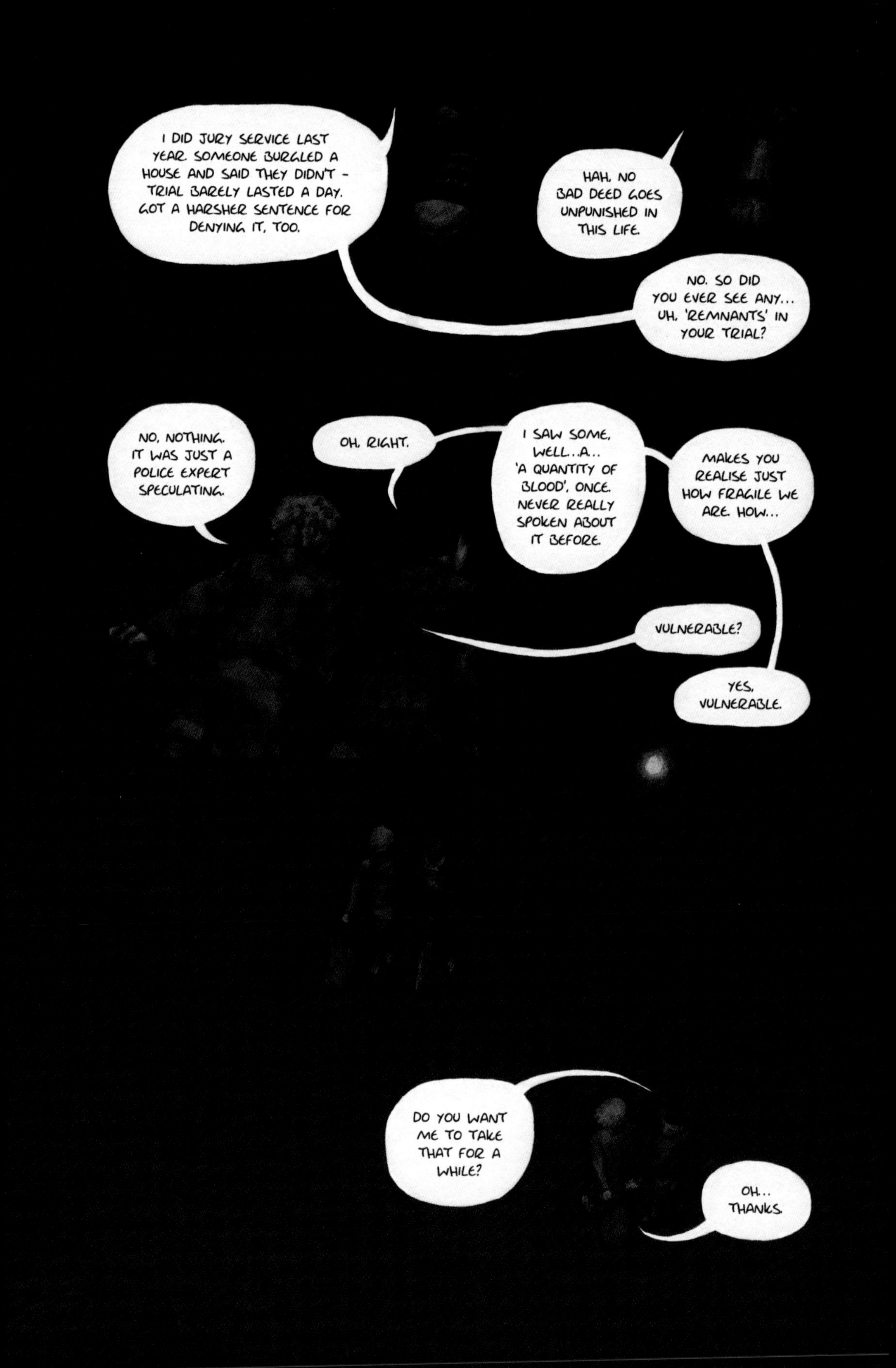
I DID JURY SERVICE LAST YEAR. SOMEONE BURGLED A HOUSE AND SAID THEY DIDN'T - TRIAL BARELY LASTED A DAY. GOT A HARSHER SENTENCE FOR DENYING IT, TOO.
HAH. NO BAD DEED GOES UNPUNISHED IN THIS LIFE.
NO. SO DID YOU EVER SEE ANY... UH, 'REMNANTS' IN YOUR TRIAL?
NO, NOTHING. IT WAS JUST A POLICE EXPERT SPECULATING.
OH, RIGHT.
I SAW SOME, WELL...A... 'A QUANTITY OF BLOOD', ONCE. NEVER REALLY SPOKEN ABOUT IT BEFORE.
MAKES YOU REALISE JUST HOW FRAGILE WE ARE. HOW...
VULNERABLE?
YES, VULNERABLE.
DO YOU WANT ME TO TAKE THAT FOR A WHILE?
OH... THANKS.

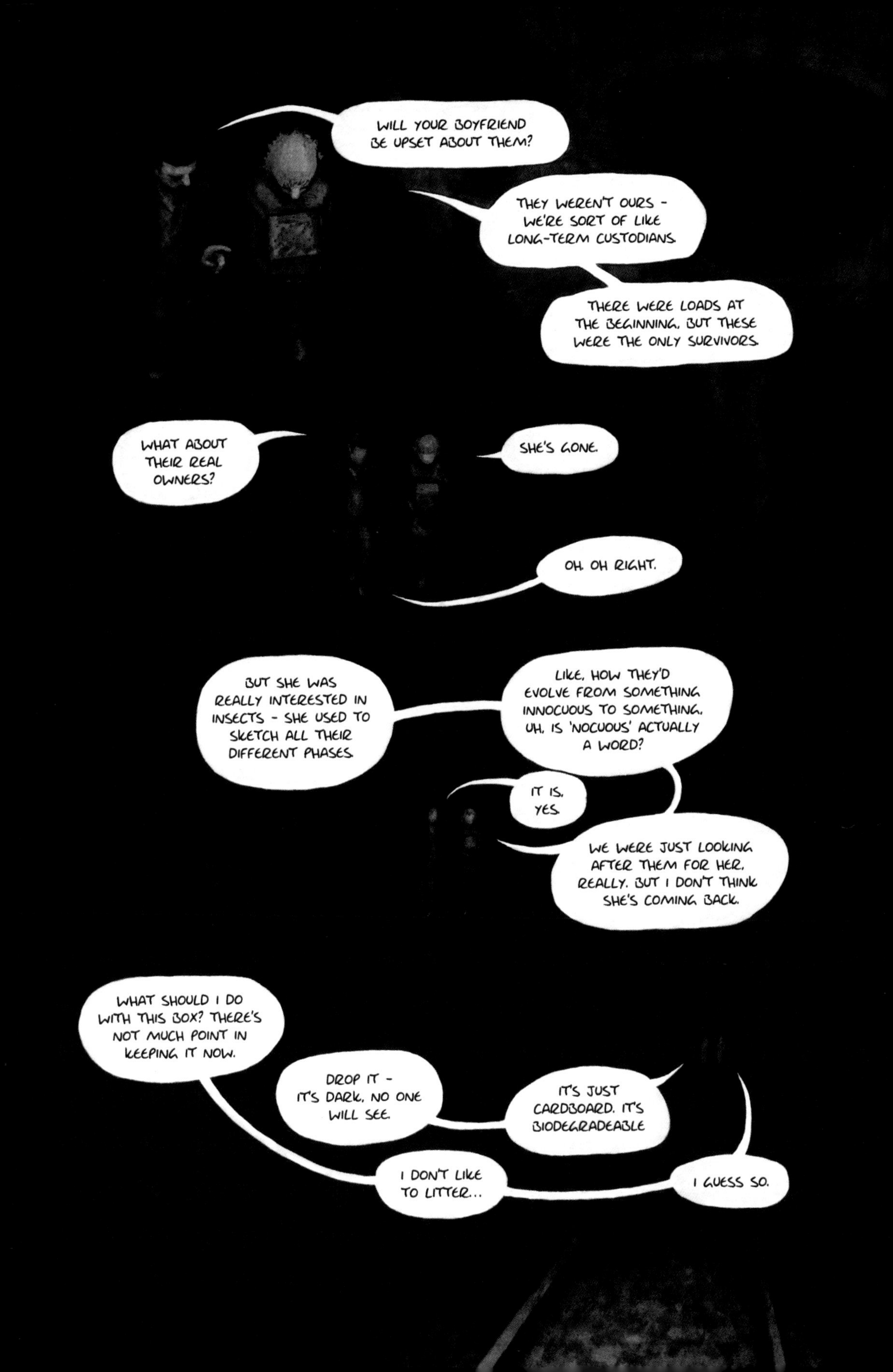
WILL YOUR BOYFRIEND BE UPSET ABOUT THEM?
THEY WEREN'T OURS - WE'RE SORT OF LIKE LONG-TERM CUSTODIANS.
THERE WERE LOADS AT THE BEGINNING, BUT THESE WERE THE ONLY SURVIVORS.
WHAT ABOUT THEIR REAL OWNERS?
SHE'S GONE.
OH. OH RIGHT.
BUT SHE WAS REALLY INTERESTED IN INSECTS - SHE USED TO SKETCH ALL THEIR DIFFERENT PHASES.
LIKE, HOW THEY'D EVOLVE FROM SOMETHING INNOCUOUS TO SOMETHING, UH, IS 'NOCUOUS' ACTUALLY A WORD?
IT IS, YES.
WE WERE JUST LOOKING AFTER THEM FOR HER, REALLY. BUT I DON'T THINK SHE'S COMING BACK.
WHAT SHOULD I DO WITH THIS BOX? THERE'S NOT MUCH POINT IN KEEPING IT NOW.
DROP IT - IT'S DARK, NO ONE WILL SEE.
IT'S JUST CARDBOARD. IT'S BIODEGRADEABLE
I DON'T LIKE TO LITTER...
I GUESS SO.

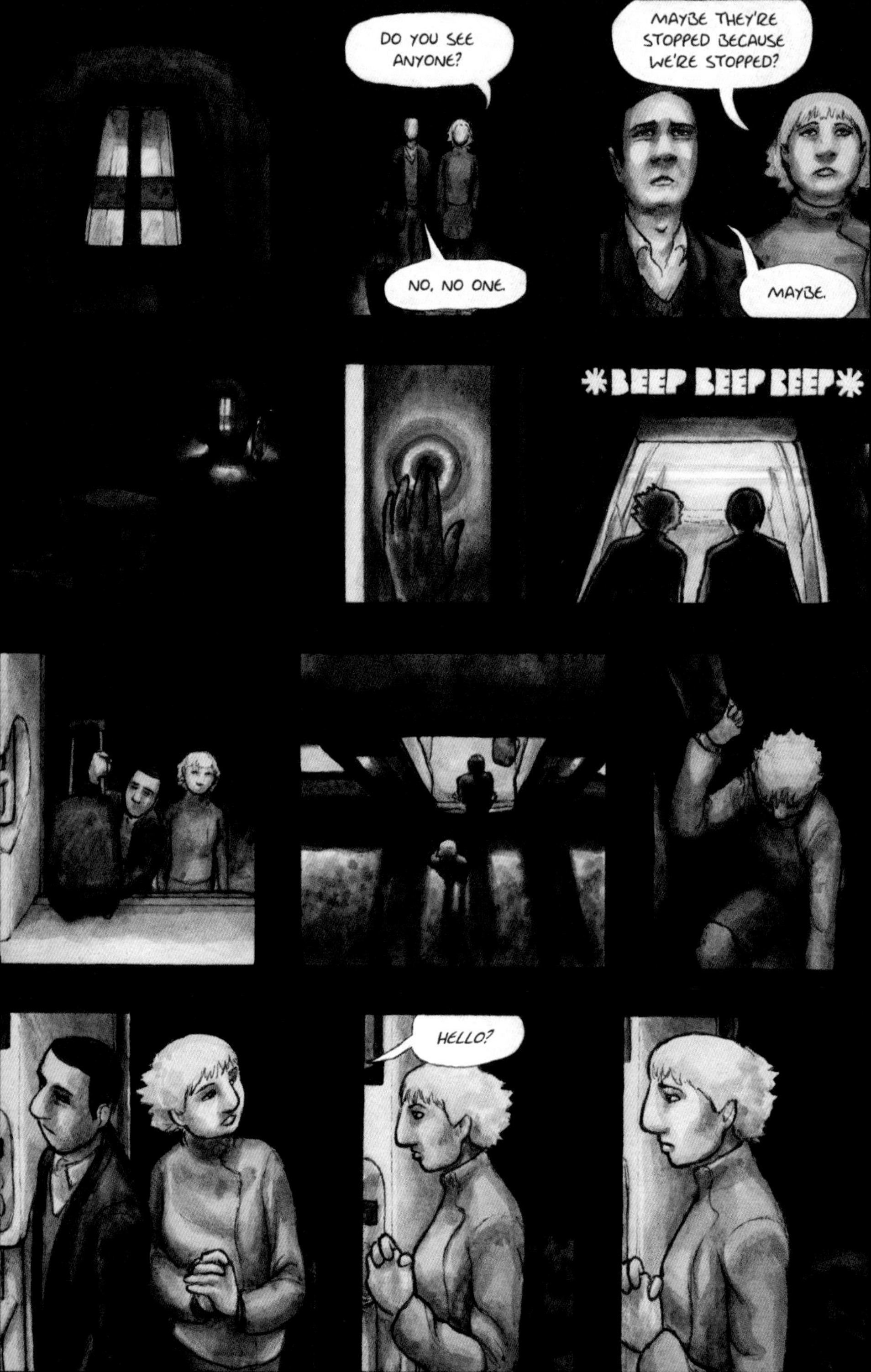
DO YOU SEE ANYONE?
NO, NO ONE.
MAYBE THEY'RE STOPPED BECAUSE WE'RE STOPPED?
MAYBE.
BEEP BEEP BEEP
HELLO?

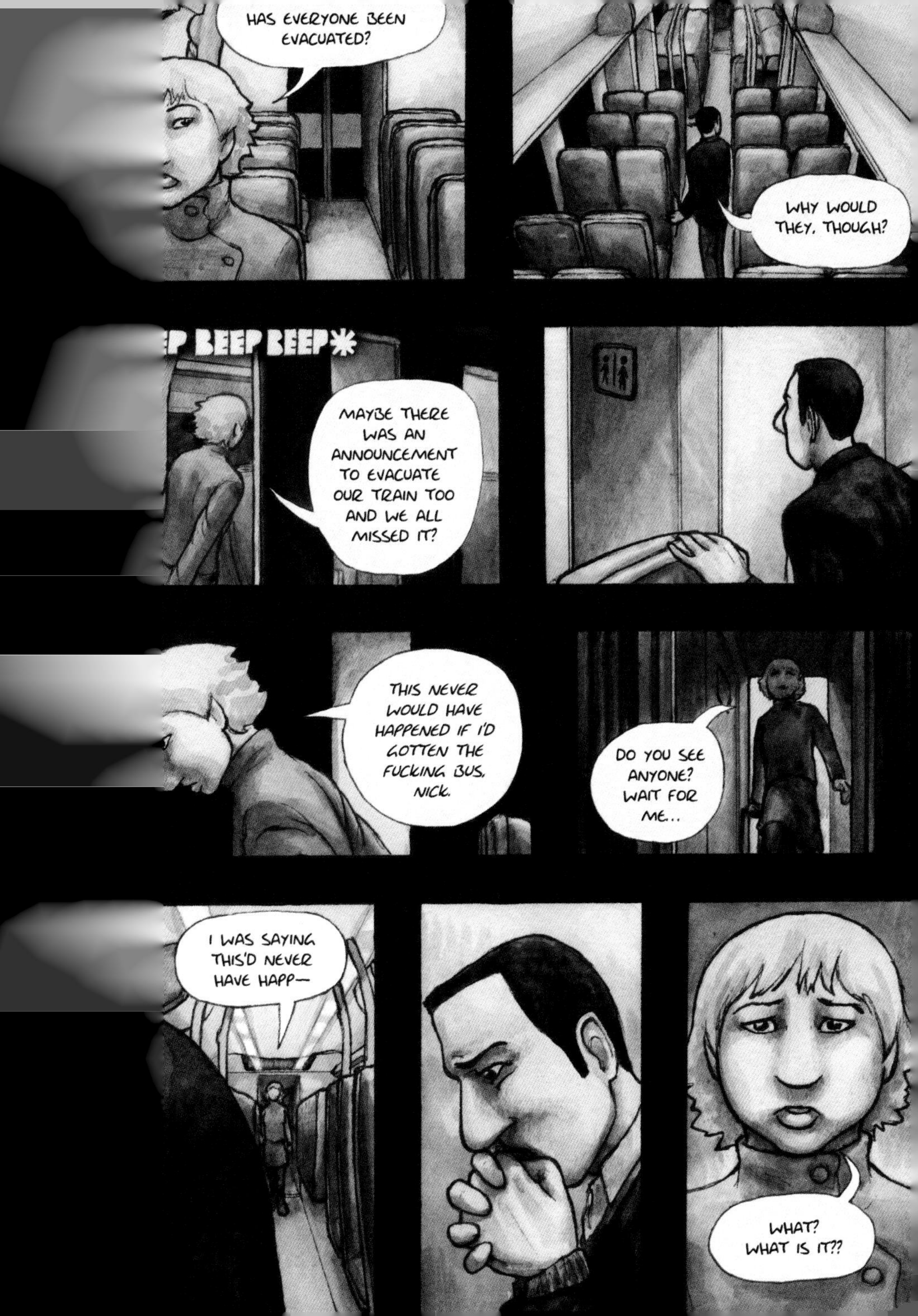
HAS EVERYONE BEEN EVACUATED?
WHY WOULD THEY, THOUGH?
P BEEP BEEP*
MAYBE THERE WAS AN ANNOUNCEMENT TO EVACUATE OUR TRAIN TOO AND WE ALL MISSED IT?
THIS NEVER WOULD HAVE HAPPENED IF I'D GOTTEN THE FUCKING BUS, NICK.
DO YOU SEE ANYONE? WAIT FOR ME...
I WAS SAYING THIS'D NEVER HAVE HAPP—
WHAT? WHAT IS IT??

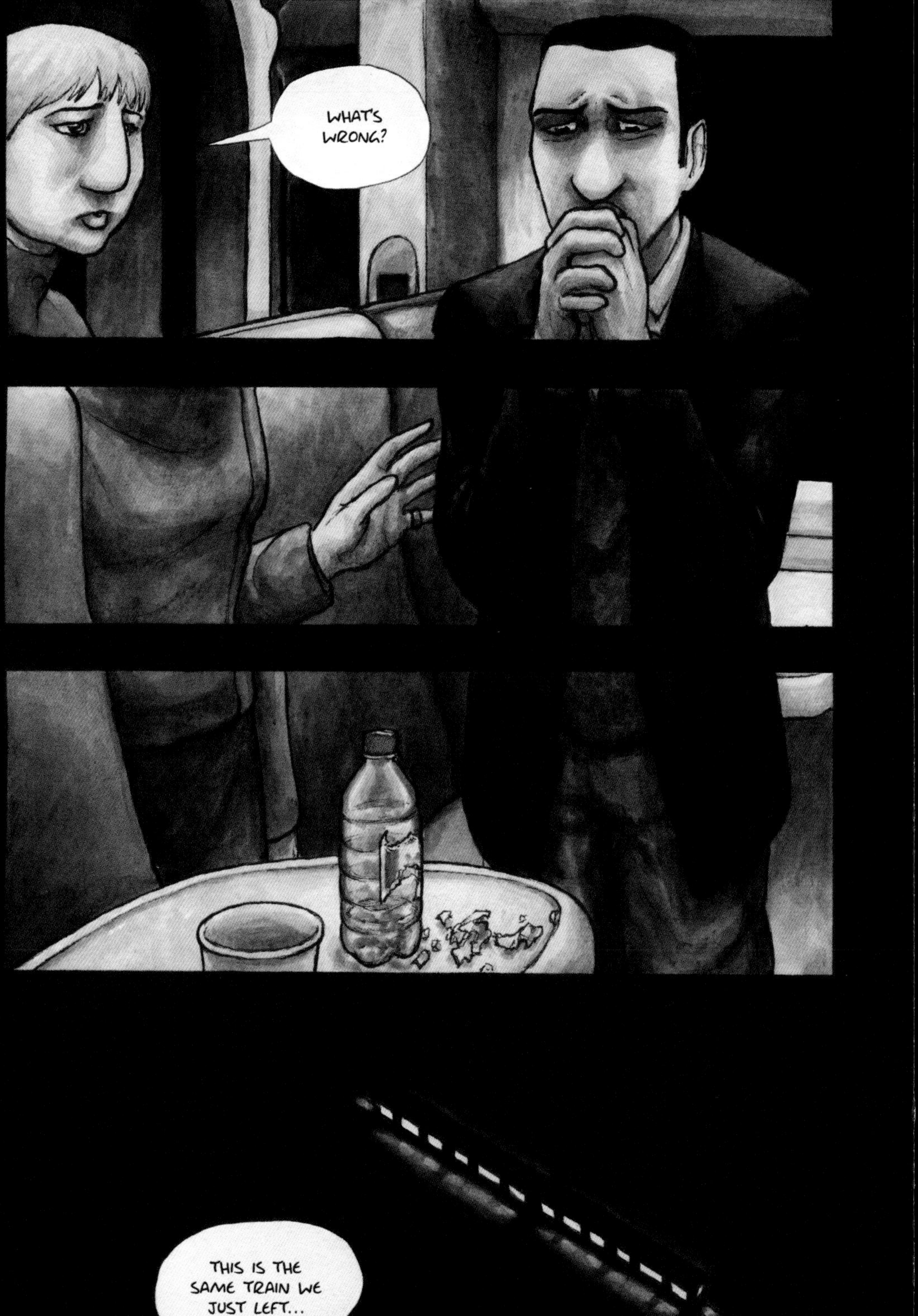
WHAT'S WRONG?
THIS IS THE SAME TRAIN WE JUST LEFT...

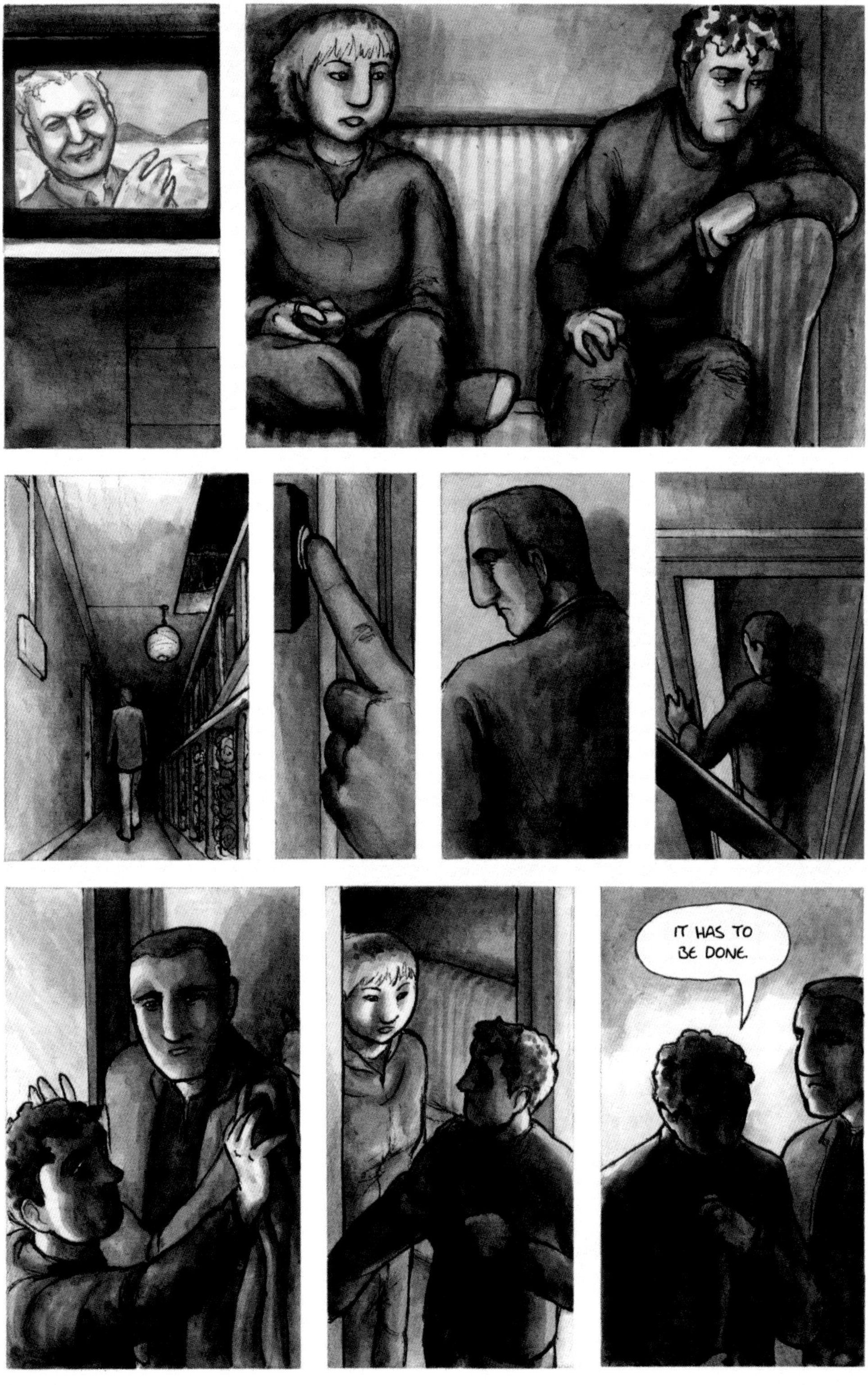
IT HAS TO BE DONE.

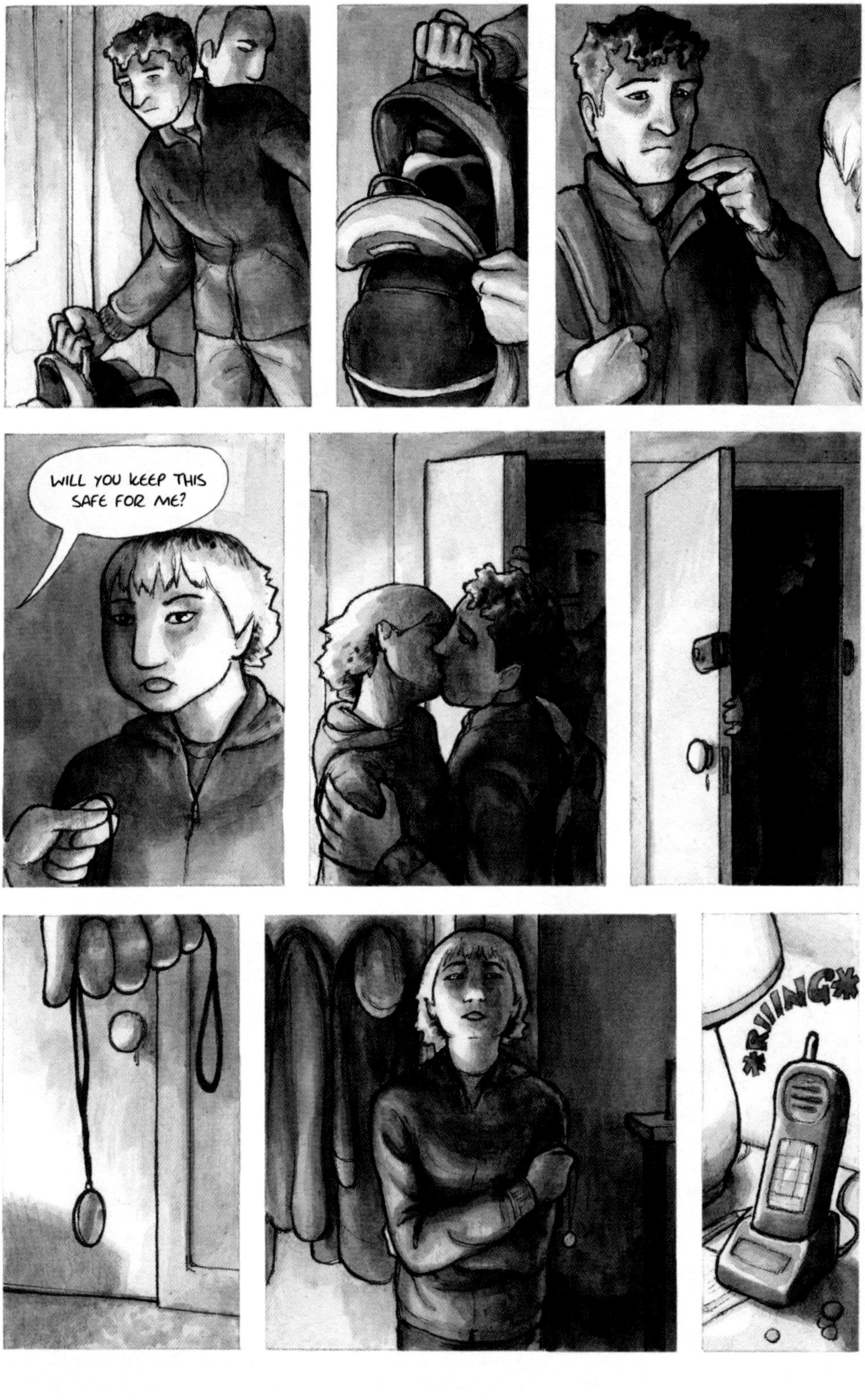
WILL YOU KEEP THIS SAFE FOR ME?
RIIING

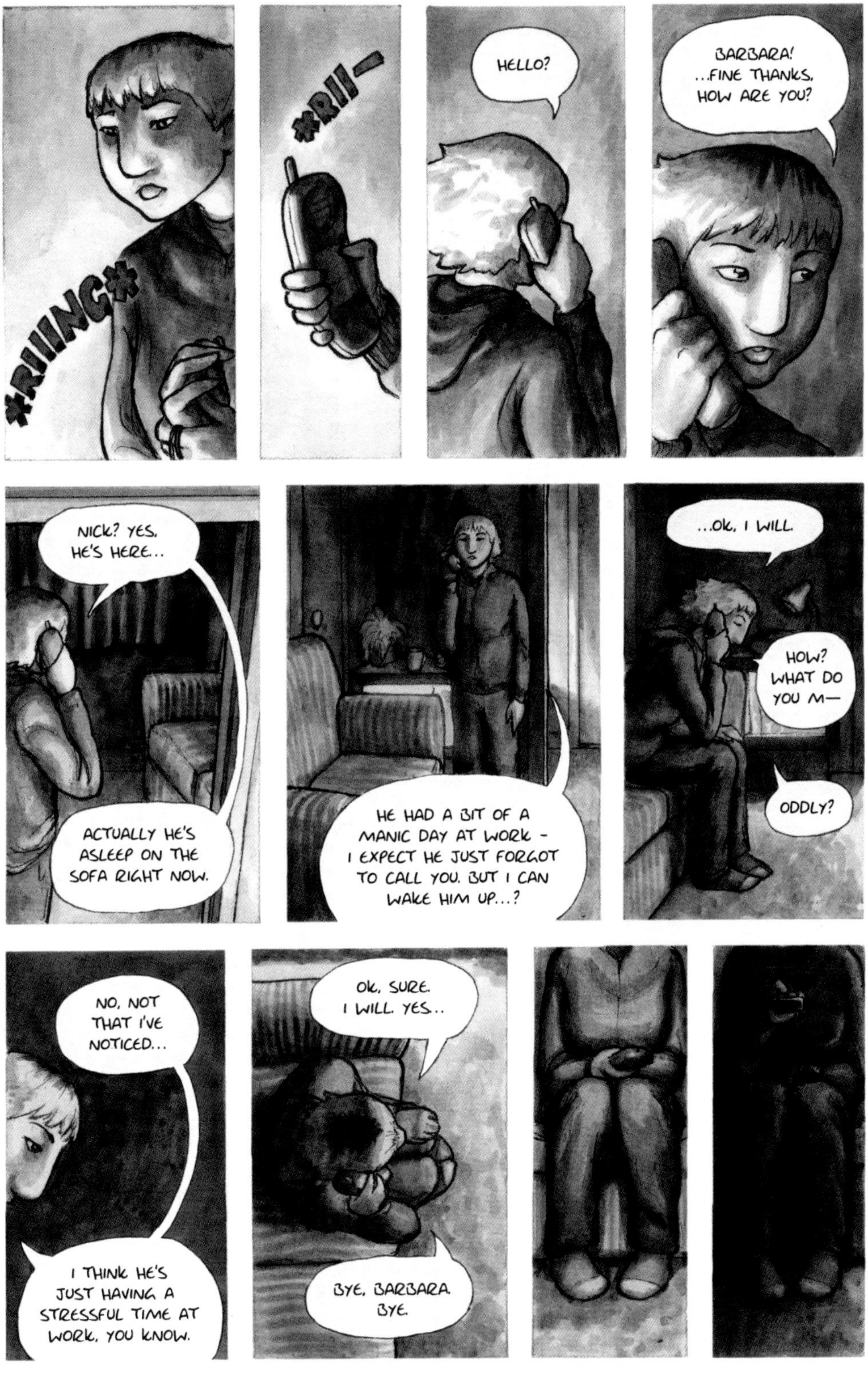
RIIING
*RII–
HELLO?
BARBARA! ...FINE THANKS, HOW ARE YOU?
NICK? YES, HE'S HERE...
ACTUALLY HE'S ASLEEP ON THE SOFA RIGHT NOW.
HE HAD A BIT OF A MANIC DAY AT WORK - I EXPECT HE JUST FORGOT TO CALL YOU. BUT I CAN WAKE HIM UP...?
...OK, I WILL.
HOW? WHAT DO YOU M—
ODDLY?
NO, NOT THAT I'VE NOTICED...
I THINK HE'S JUST HAVING A STRESSFUL TIME AT WORK, YOU KNOW.
OK, SURE. I WILL. YES...
BYE, BARBARA. BYE.

ARE YOU SURE??

YES

THAT'S NOT POSSIBLE. IT'S NOT. THIS...

IT'S A JOKE, ISN'T IT.

THIS CAN'T BE A JOKE. IT'S NOT FUNNY.

EVERYTHING IS FUNNY TO SOMEONE...

IT'S A TRICK, SOMETHING FOR THE TELLY:

THEY'VE MOVED THE TRAIN AHEAD OF US, SOMEHOW... OR...

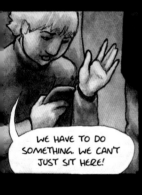

WE HAVE TO DO SOMETHING. WE CAN'T JUST SIT HERE!

WE HAVE TO DO SOMETHING!

OK. OK THEN. ALRIGHT.

YOU CAN'T SMOKE ON HERE.

EXACTLY! WE'LL SEE IF THIS IS A JOKE. THEY CAN IMPRISON US AND TORMENT US IN THE NAME OF LIGHT ENTERTAINMENT, BUT THEY CAN'T HAVE US SMOKING INDOORS...

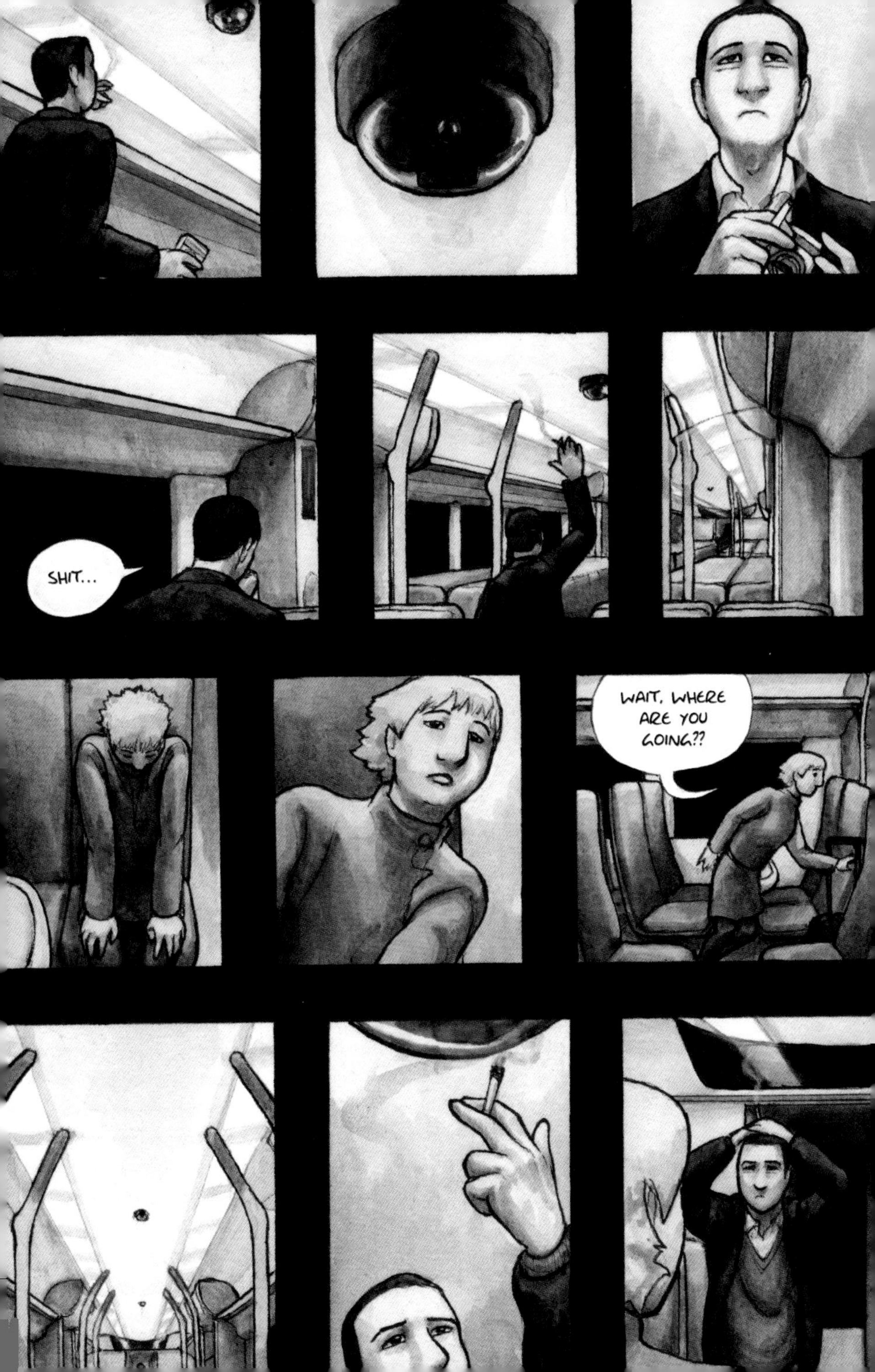
SHIT...
WAIT, WHERE ARE YOU GOING??

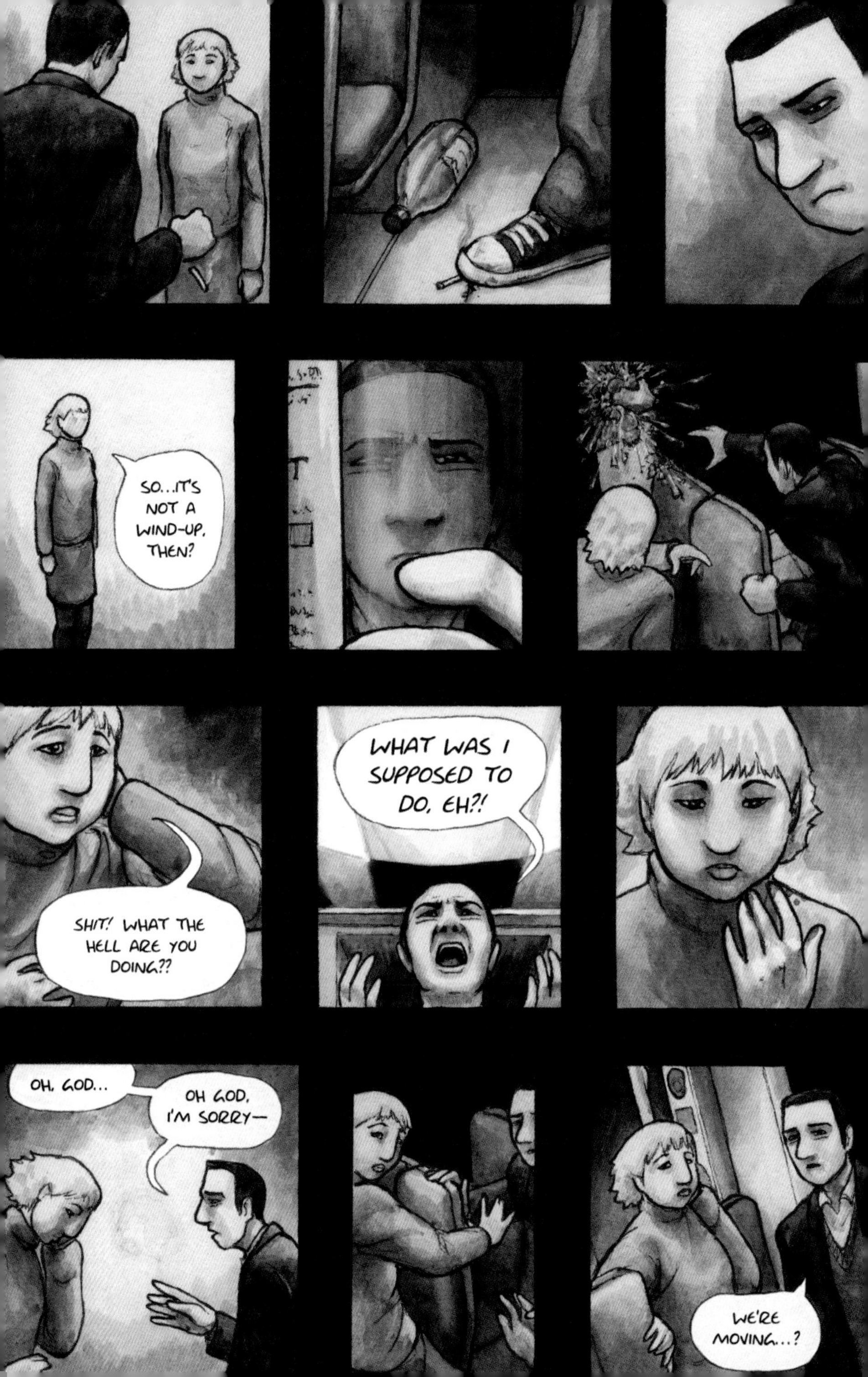
SO...IT'S NOT A WIND-UP, THEN?
SHIT! WHAT THE HELL ARE YOU DOING??
WHAT WAS I SUPPOSED TO DO, EH?!
OH, GOD...
OH GOD, I'M SORRY—
WE'RE MOVING...?

THIS IS A WIND-UP?

HOW CAN WE BE MOVING, THOUGH?

DON'T KNOW. WIRES? SOMETHING WE COULDN'T SEE IN THE DARK.

ARE YOU OKAY?

I WANT TO GO HOME.

IT'S FOR TV. IT MUST BE.

THAT OTHER WOMAN... THAT'S WHY SHE WAS SO ABRASIVE -

SHE WAS TRYING TO GET ME TO REACT; BE AN ARSEHOLE FOR THE CAMERAS...

RIGHT?

I SHOULD'VE REALISED—

WAIT, ARE YOU IN ON ALL THIS??

ARE YOU... IS THIS A TRAP?

A TRAP? A TRAP FOR WHAT? FOR YOU? WHY WOULD SOMEONE SET A TRAP FOR YOU?

NOT... NOT FOR ME...

ALTHOUGH YOU WOULDN'T TELL ME IF IT WAS AND IF YOU

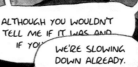
WE'RE SLOWING DOWN ALREADY.

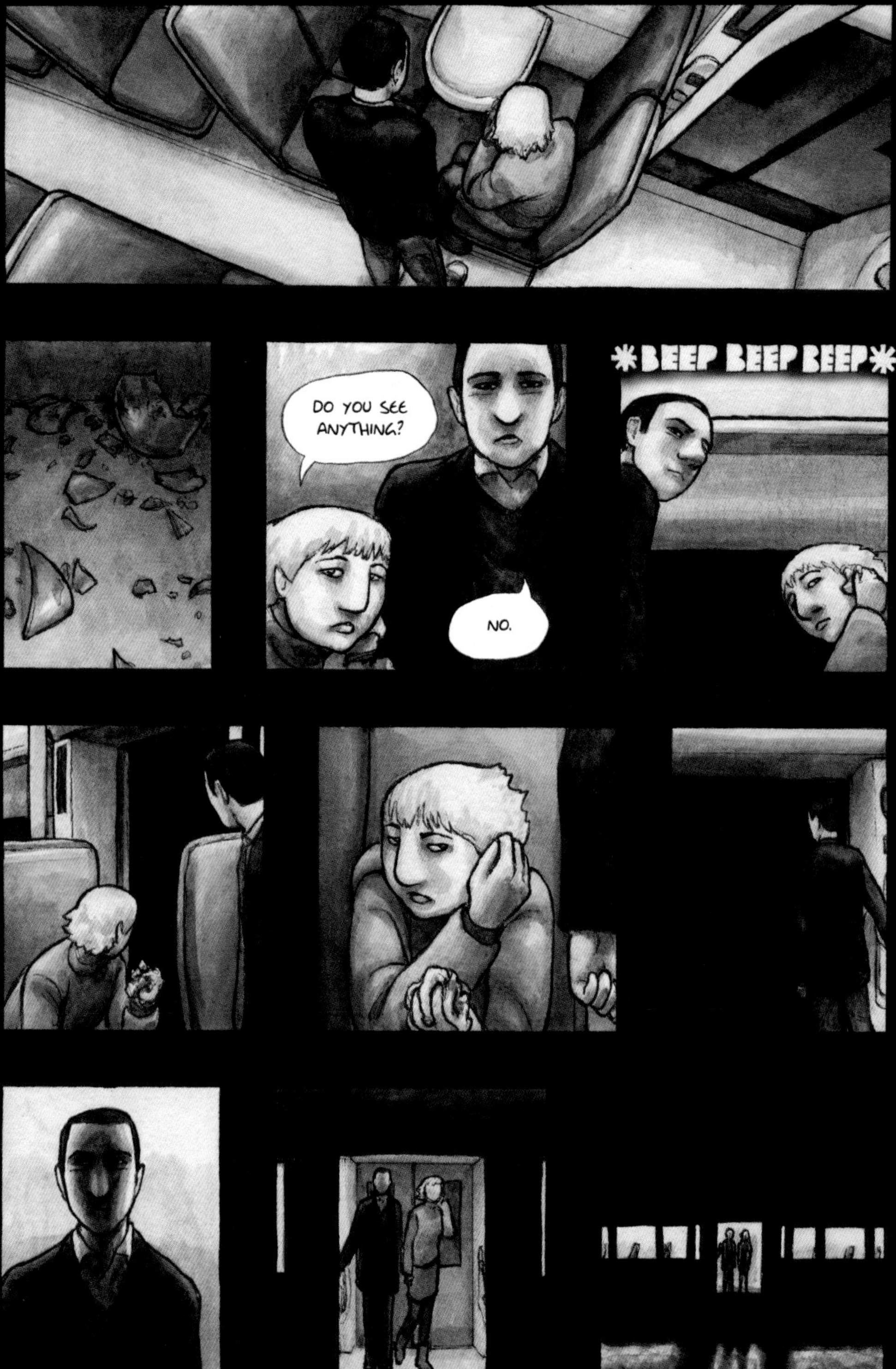
DO YOU SEE ANYTHING?
NO.
BEEP BEEP BEEP

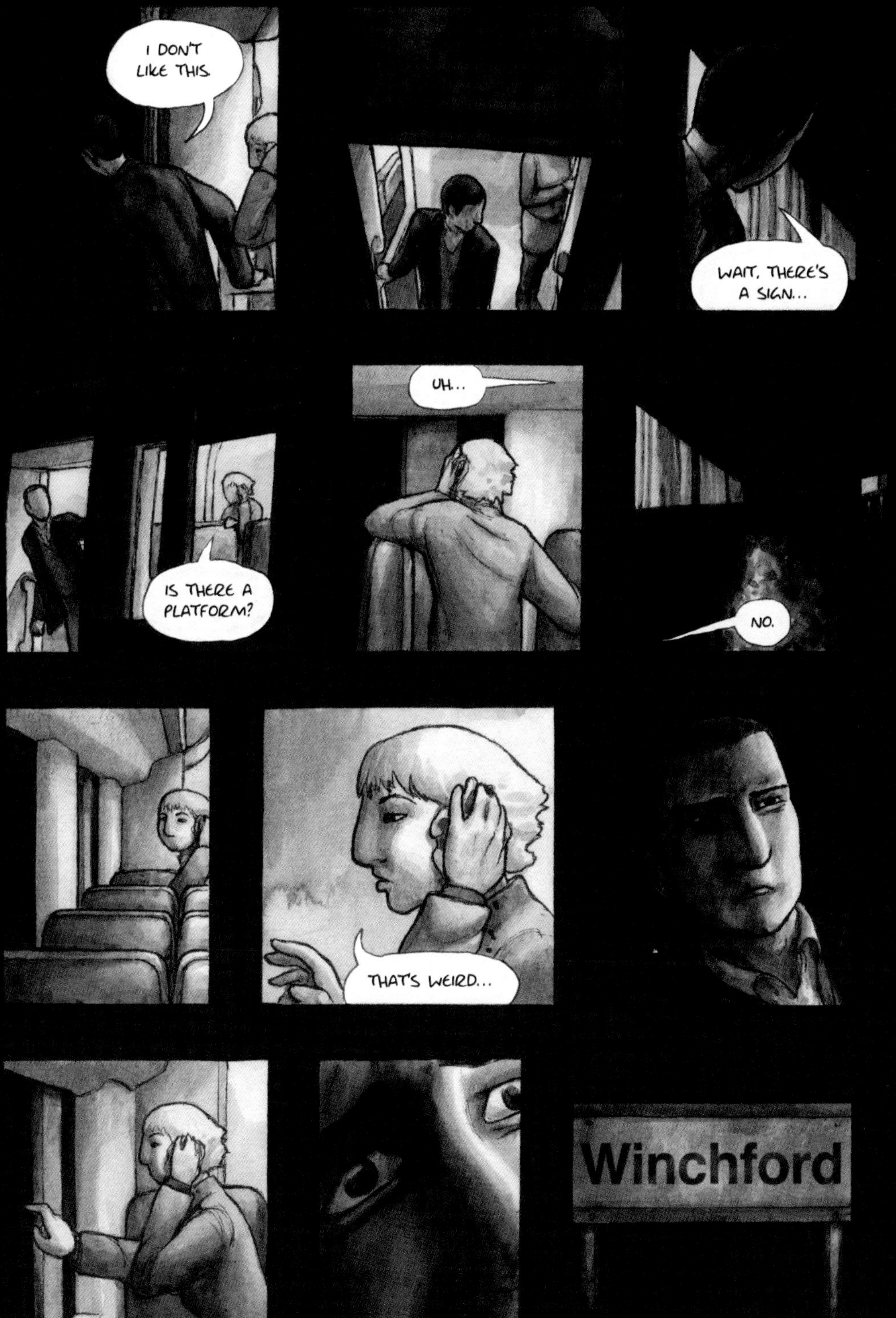
I DON'T LIKE THIS.
WAIT, THERE'S A SIGN...
UH...
IS THERE A PLATFORM?
NO.
THAT'S WEIRD...
Winchford

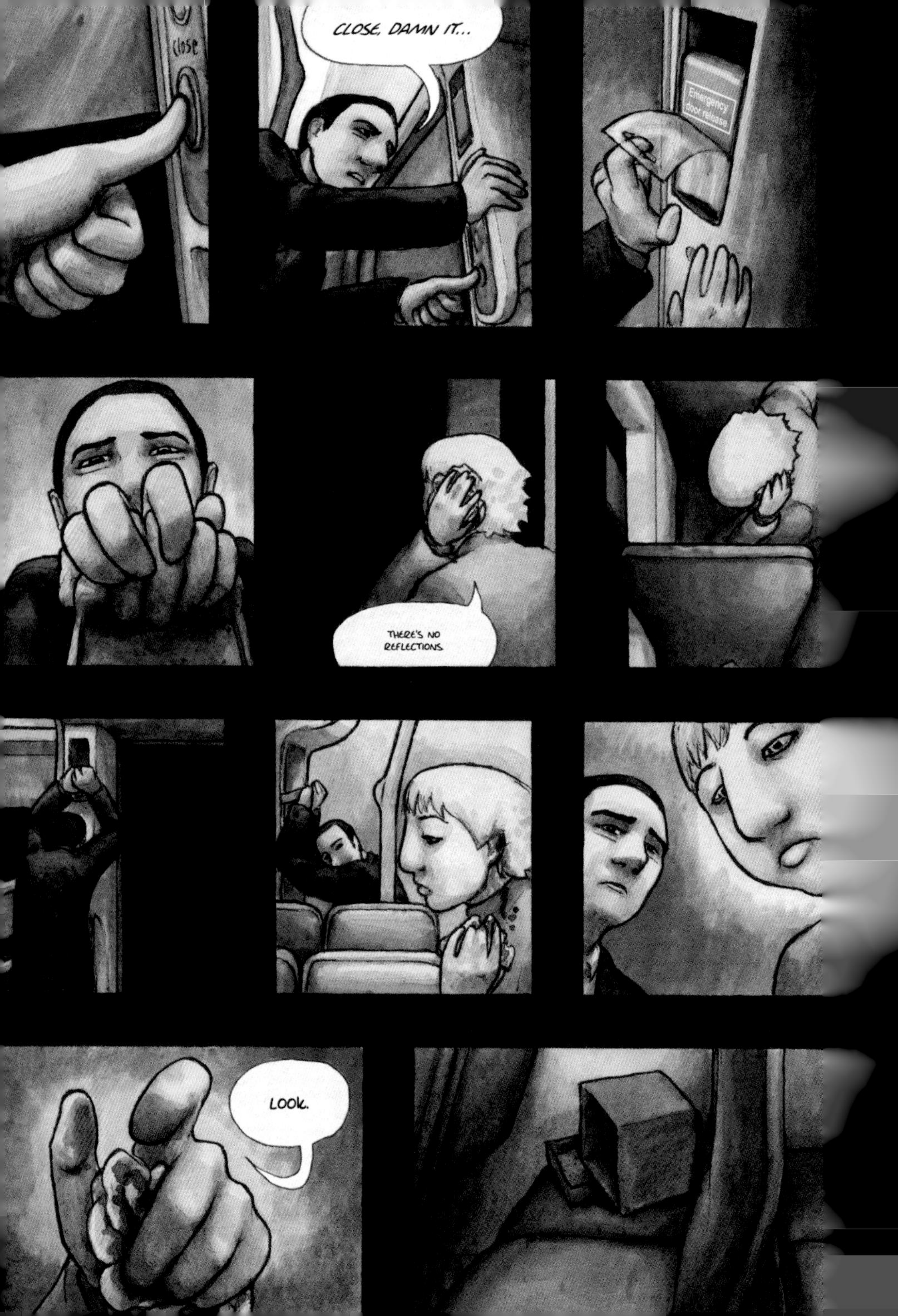

close
CLOSE, DAMN IT...
Emergency door release
THERE'S NO REFLECTIONS.
LOOK.

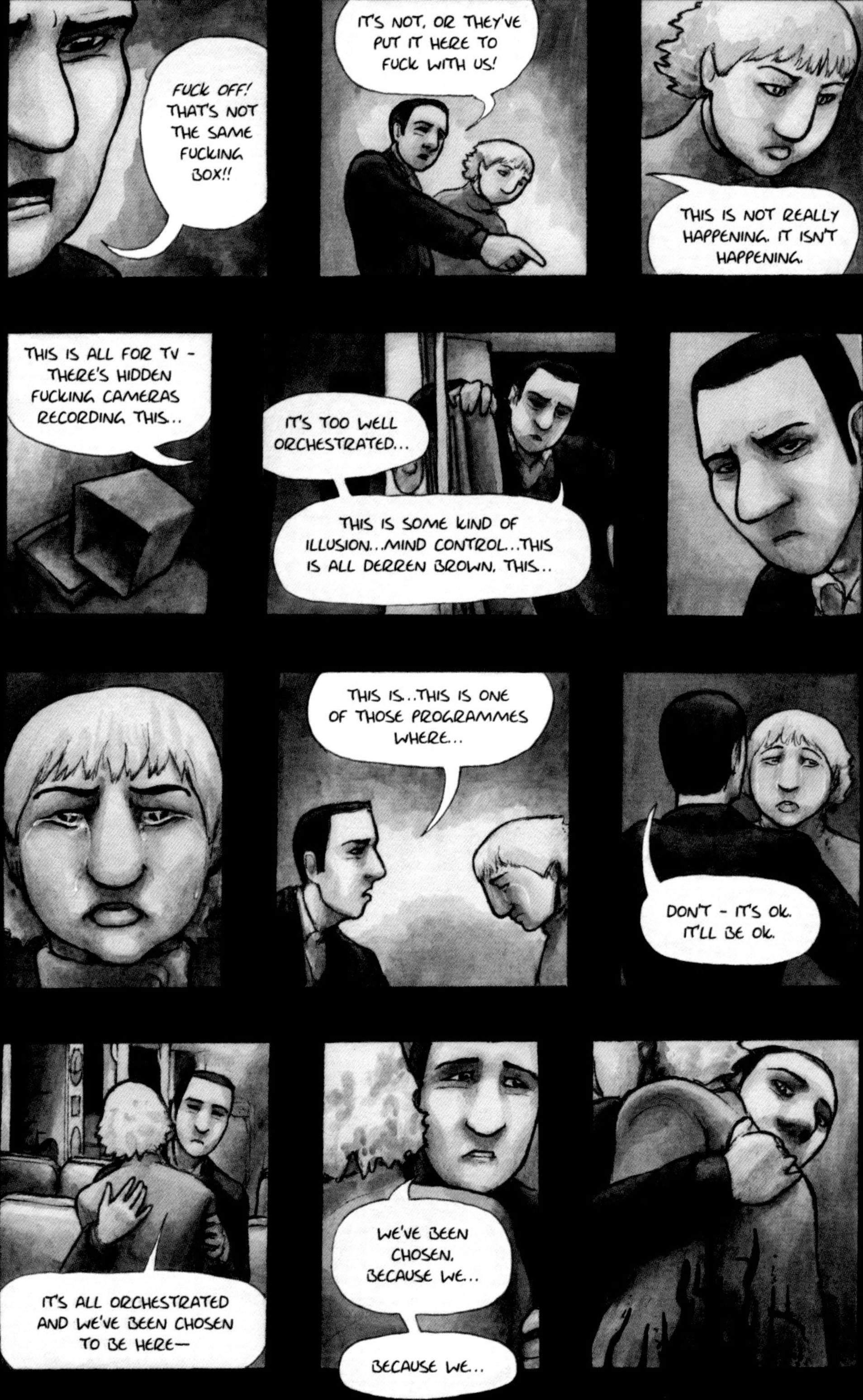
FUCK OFF! THAT'S NOT THE SAME FUCKING BOX!!
IT'S NOT, OR THEY'VE PUT IT HERE TO FUCK WITH US!
THIS IS NOT REALLY HAPPENING. IT ISN'T HAPPENING.
THIS IS ALL FOR TV - THERE'S HIDDEN FUCKING CAMERAS RECORDING THIS..
IT'S TOO WELL ORCHESTRATED...
THIS IS SOME KIND OF ILLUSION...MIND CONTROL...THIS IS ALL DERREN BROWN, THIS..
THIS IS...THIS IS ONE OF THOSE PROGRAMMES WHERE...
DON'T - IT'S OK. IT'LL BE OK.
IT'S ALL ORCHESTRATED AND WE'VE BEEN CHOSEN TO BE HERE—
WE'VE BEEN CHOSEN. BECAUSE WE...
BECAUSE WE...

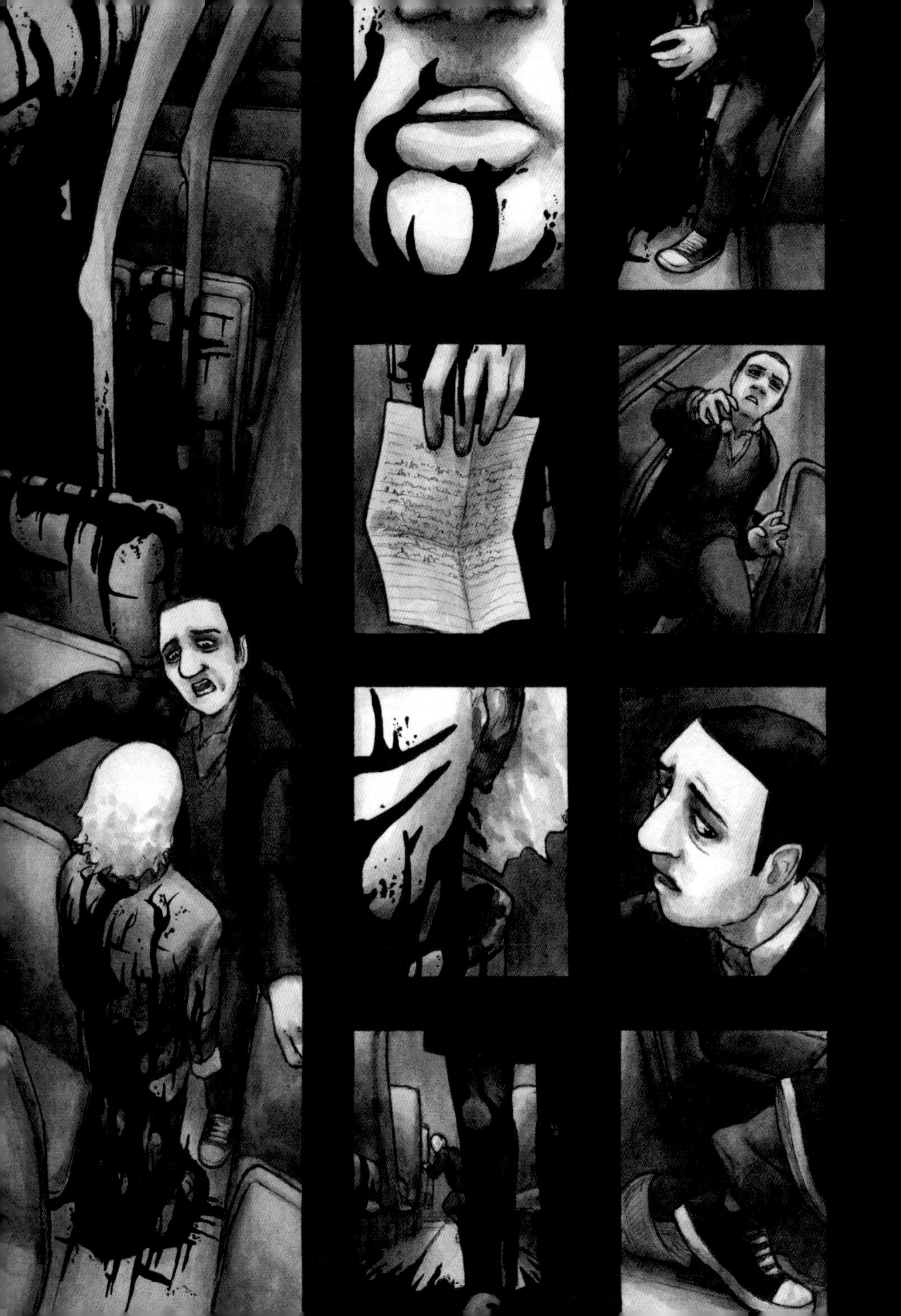

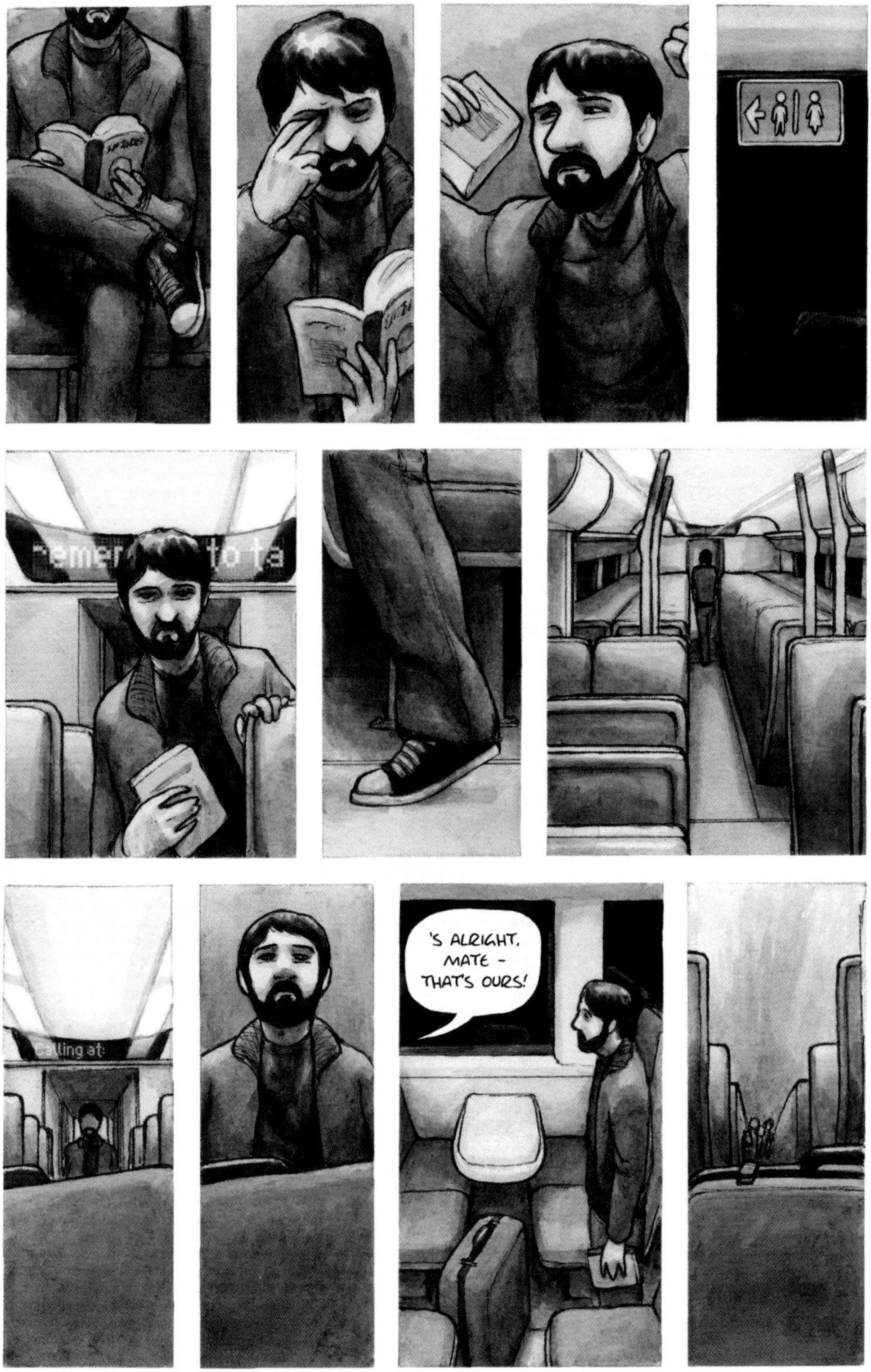
calling at:
'S ALRIGHT, MATE - THAT'S OURS!

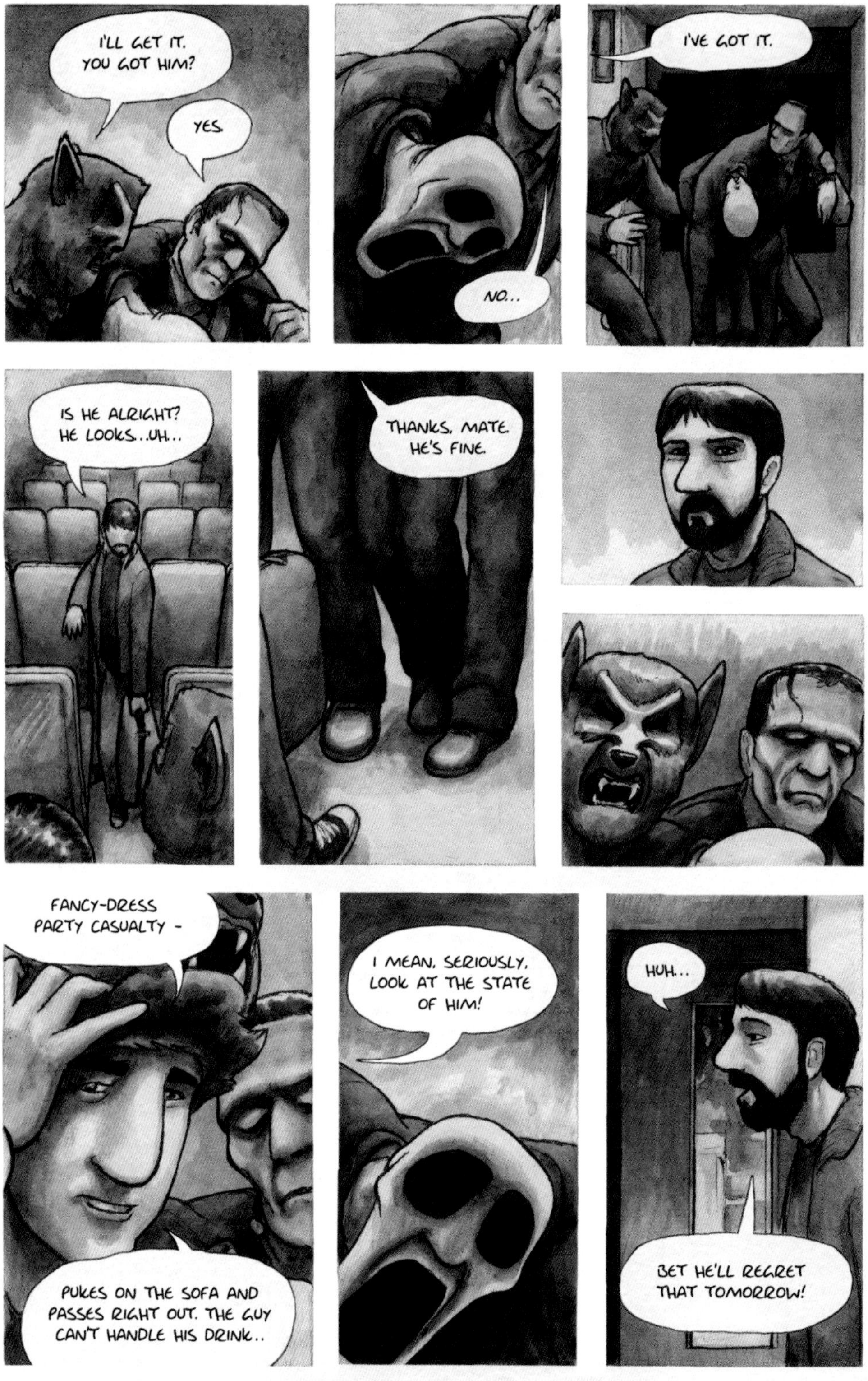
I'LL GET IT. YOU GOT HIM?
YES.
NO...
I'VE GOT IT.
IS HE ALRIGHT? HE LOOKS...UH...
THANKS, MATE. HE'S FINE.
FANCY-DRESS PARTY CASUALTY -
PUKES ON THE SOFA AND PASSES RIGHT OUT. THE GUY CAN'T HANDLE HIS DRINK..
I MEAN, SERIOUSLY, LOOK AT THE STATE OF HIM!
HUH...
BET HE'LL REGRET THAT TOMORROW!

NO DOUBT...

BEEP BEEP BEEP

HOLD HIM.
I'LL...TAKE THIS TO
THE TAXI.

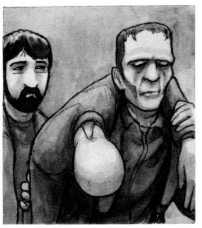

WHAT ARE YOU,
PSYCHOPATHS?

WHAT?

THE MASKS, THE
BOILER SUITS: YOU ALL
WENT TO THE PARTY AS
PSYCHOPATHS, RIGHT?
LIKE IN THAT FILM?

YEAH. YES.

Winchford

HELP
ME

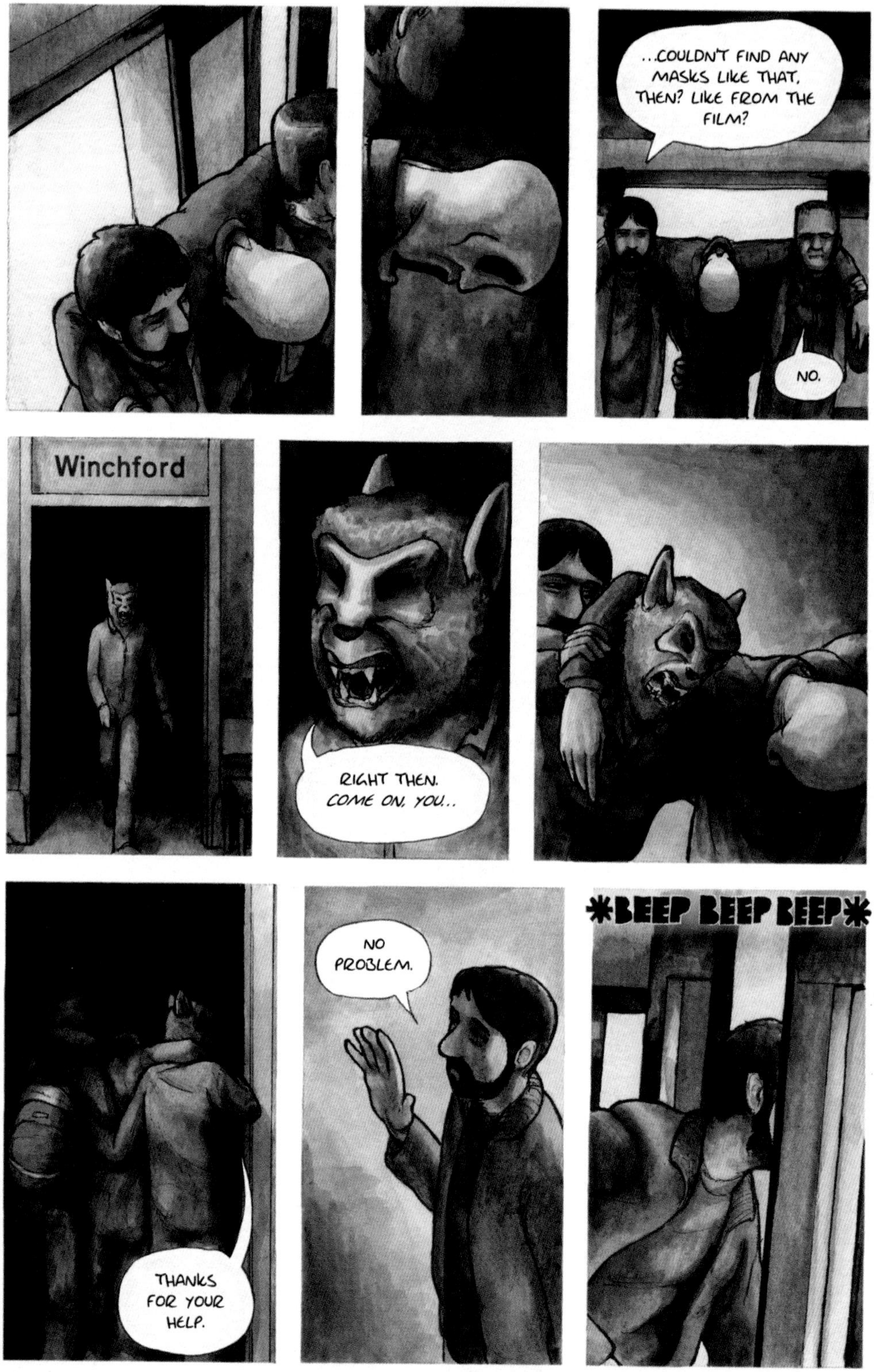
...COULDN'T FIND ANY MASKS LIKE THAT, THEN? LIKE FROM THE FILM?
NO.
Winchford
RIGHT THEN. COME ON, YOU...
THANKS FOR YOUR HELP.
NO PROBLEM.
BEEP BEEP BEEP

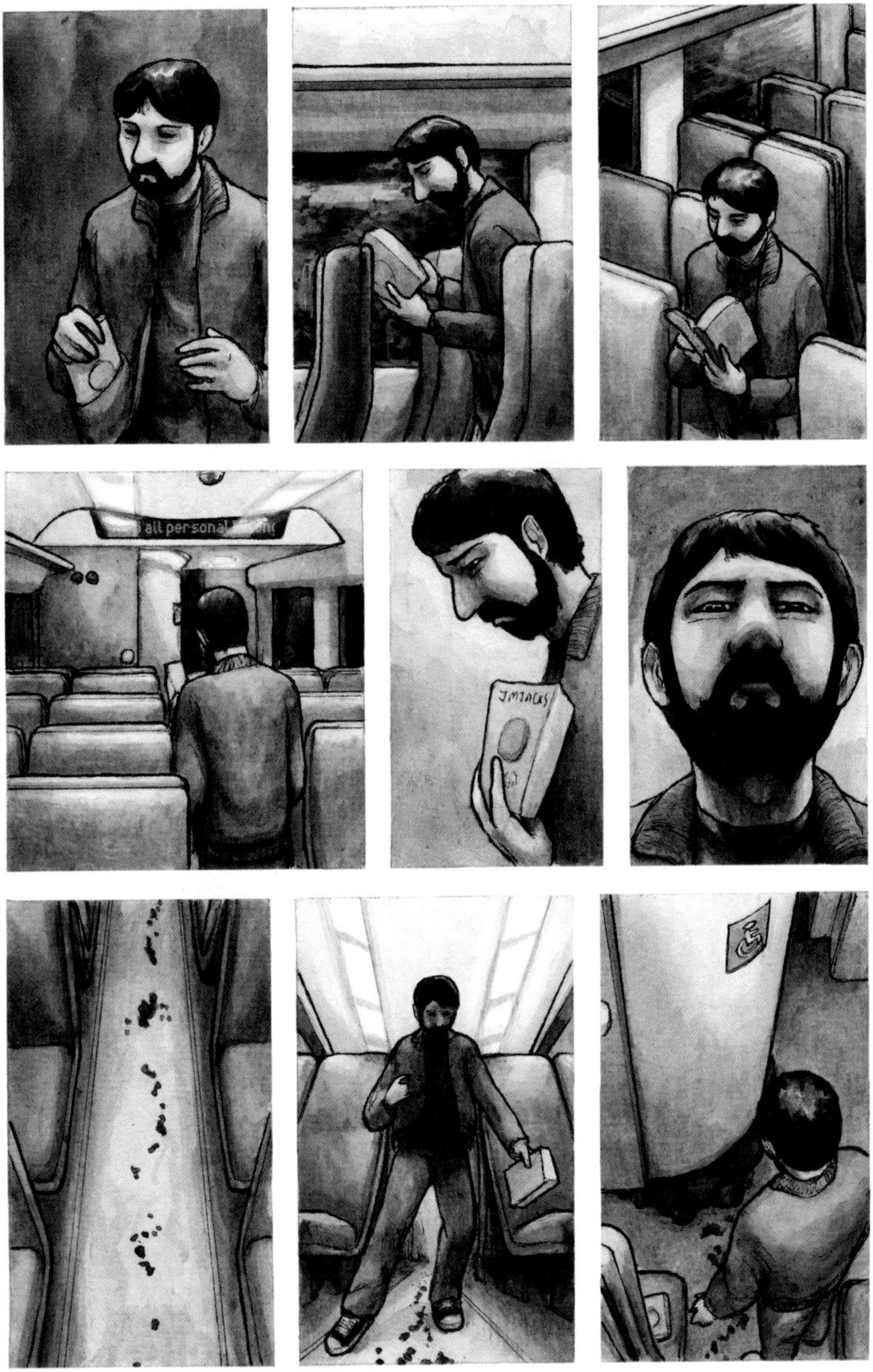
all personal
JMJACKS

QANTAS
MOON/RODNEY MR
LONDON
NAME
MOON/
Calling...
999
End call

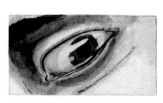

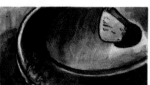

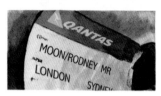

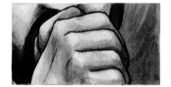

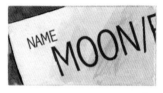

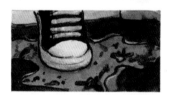

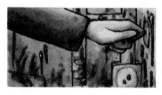

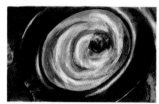

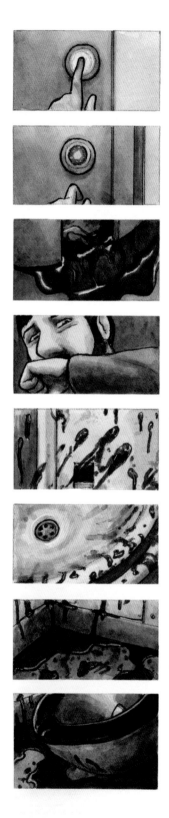

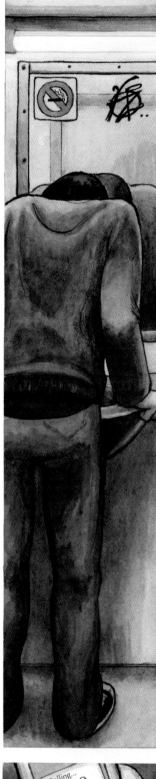

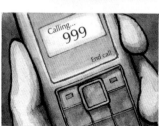

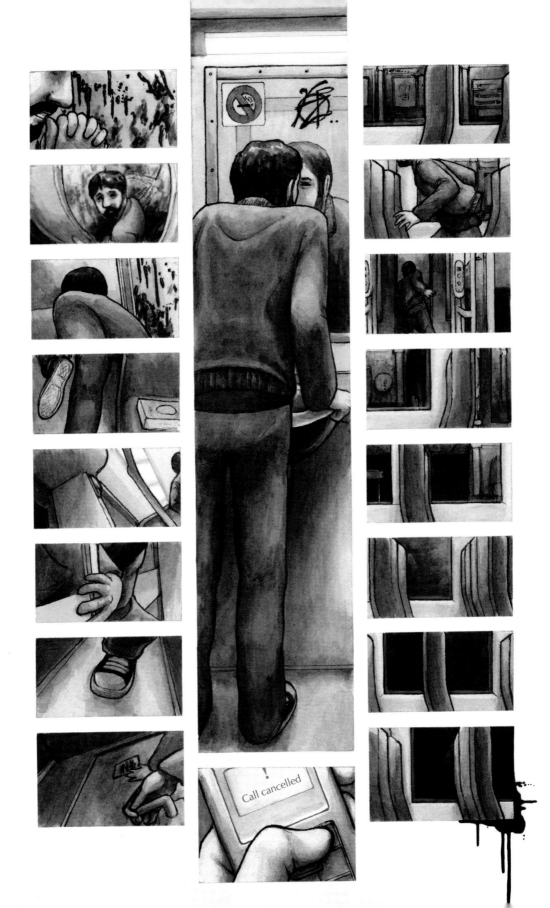

Call cancelled

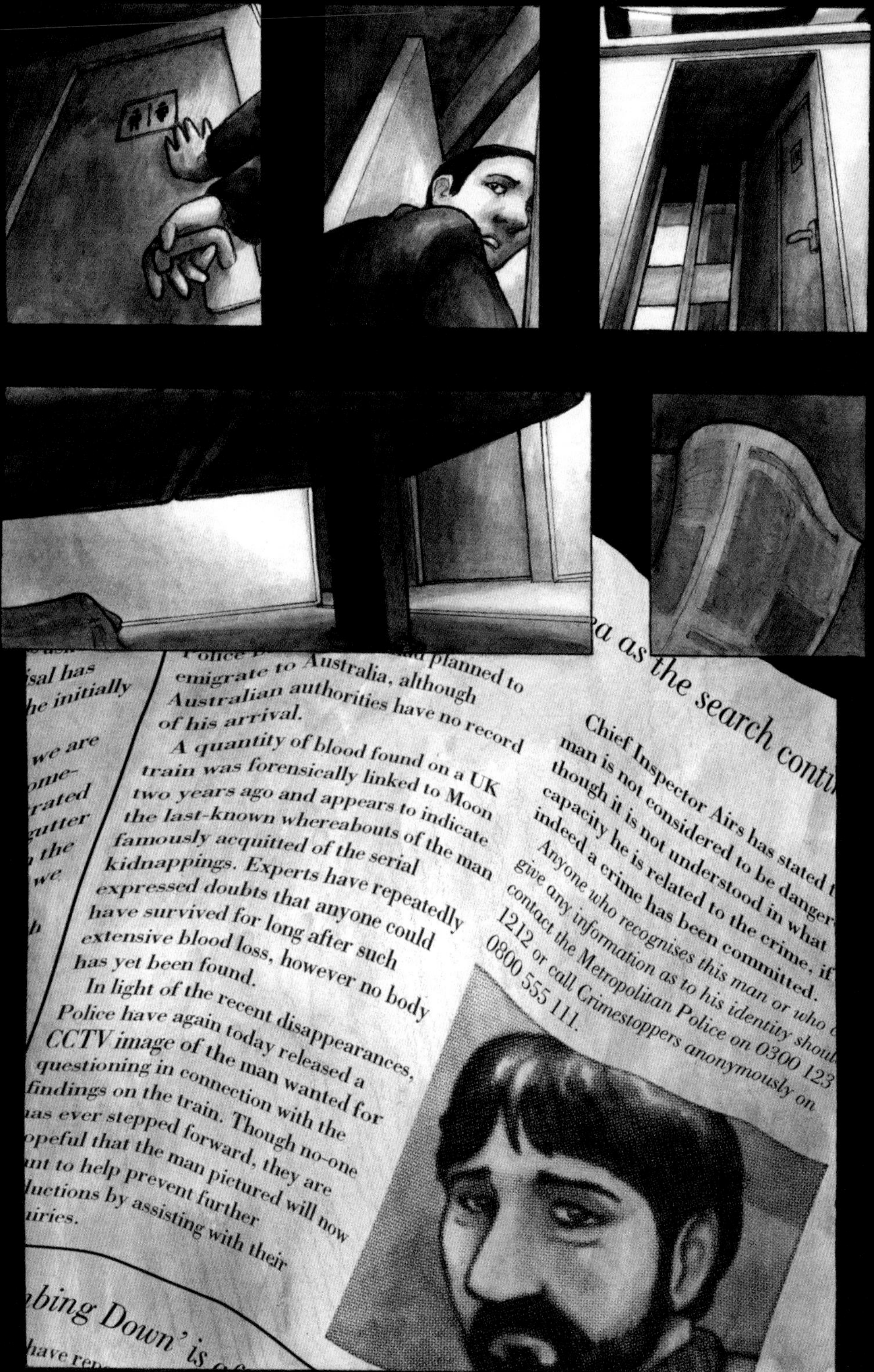

emigrate to Australia, although
Australian authorities have no record
of his arrival.
A quantity of blood found on a UK
train was forensically linked to Moon
two years ago and appears to indicate
the last-known whereabouts of the man
famously acquitted of the serial
kidnappings. Experts have repeatedly
expressed doubts that anyone could
have survived for long after such
extensive blood loss, however no body
has yet been found.
In light of the recent disappearances,
Police have again today released a
CCTV image of the man wanted for
questioning in connection with the
findings on the train. Though no-one
stepped forward, they are
that the man pictured will now
to help prevent further
by assisting with their
as the search
Chief Inspector Airs has stated
man is not considered to be
though it is not understood in what
capacity he is related to the crime, if
indeed a crime has been committed.
Anyone who recognises this man or who
give any information as to his identity
contact the Metropolitan Police on 0300 123
1212 or call Crimestoppers anonymously on
0800 555 111.
Down' is

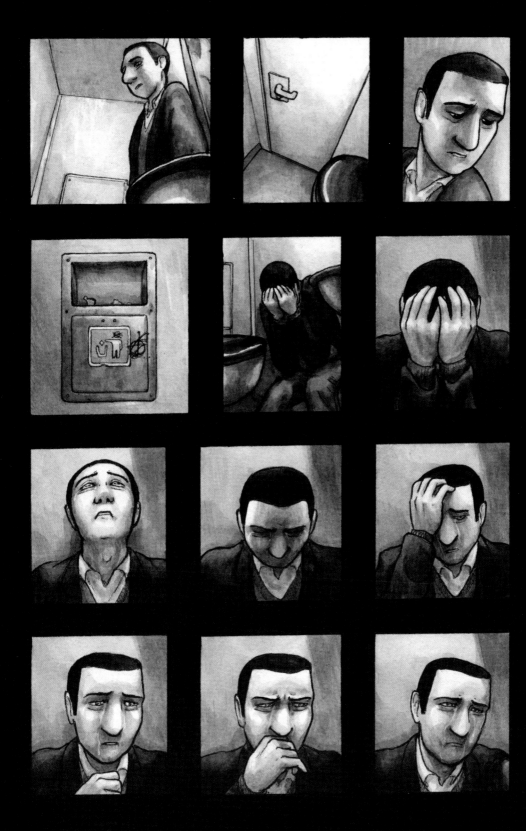

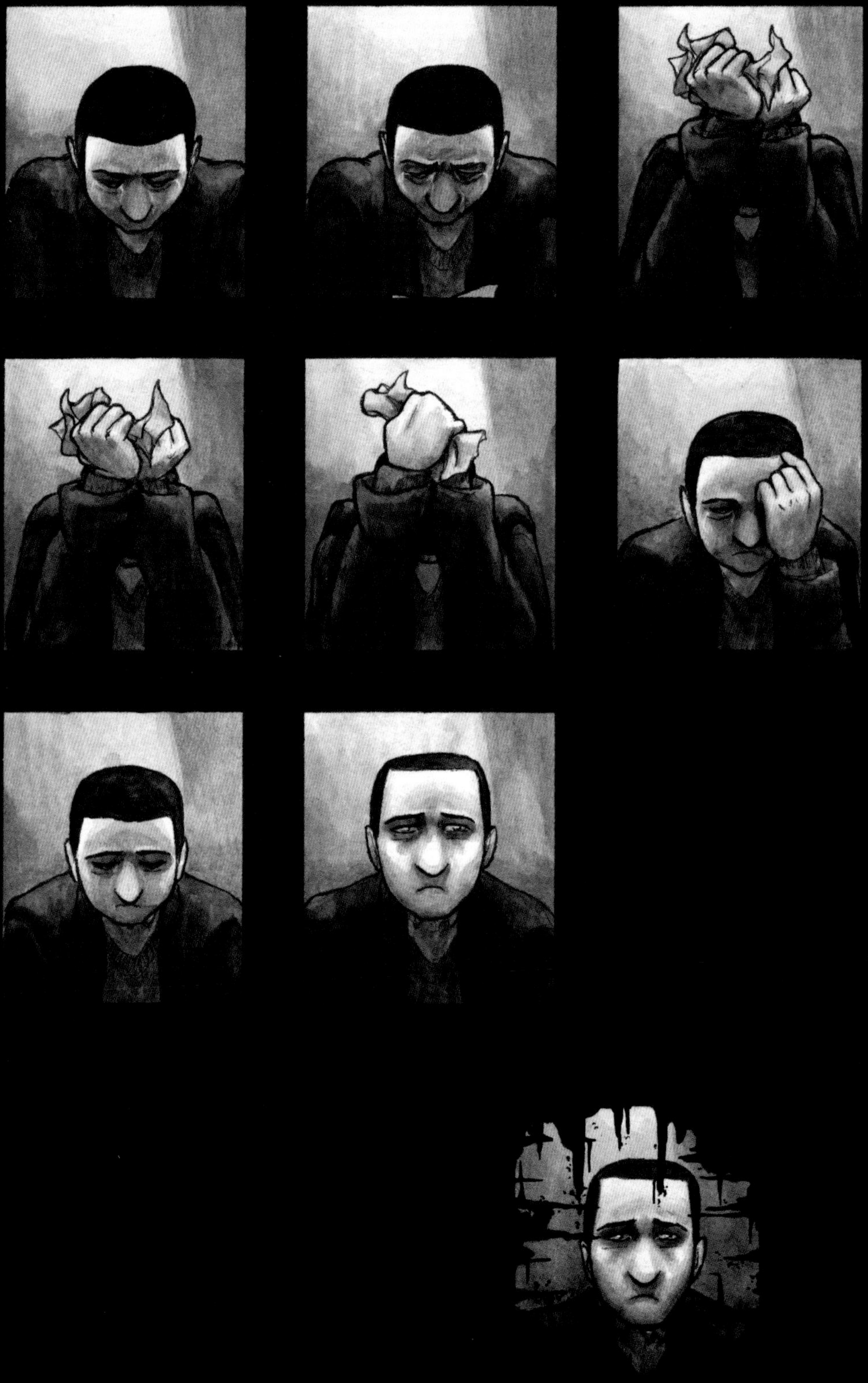

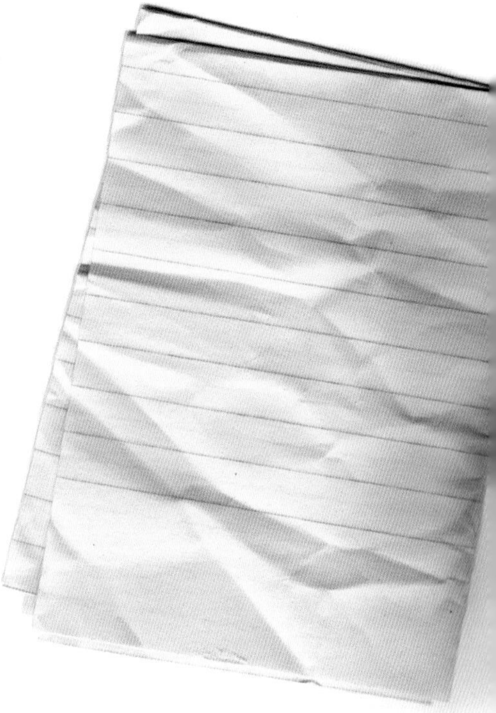